QUIVIRA SOCIETY
PUBLICATIONS

Managing Editor
GEORGE P. HAMMOND

VOLUME XIII

ARNO PRESS
NEW YORK
1967

THE FRONTIERS OF NEW SPAIN

NICOLAS DE LAFORA'S DESCRIPTION
1766-1768

LAWRENCE KINNAIRD

THE QUIVIRA SOCIETY

BERKELEY, 1958

First Published by
THE QUIVIRA SOCIETY
1958

•

Republished by
Arno Press
1967

•

Library of Congress Catalog Card
Number: 67–24724

•

Manufactured in the U.S.A.
Arno Press Inc.
New York

To
LUCIA

Preface

The delimitation of New Spain's northern frontier in 1772 was a momentous event in North American history. It was an official recognition of a fact that had been well known for many years. From the Gulf of California to the Gulf of Mexico the Spanish conquest had ceased. The Apache tribes, whose habitat extended from the valley of the Gila to the borders of Louisiana, had halted the northward Spanish advance and in many places had pushed back the frontier line of settlement.

In Spain's great reorganization following the Seven Years' War, the Marqués de Rubí surveyed the frontier defenses and proposed the creation of a cordon of presidios along the entire northern limits of the viceroyalty of New Spain. He made this tour of inspection in the years 1766-1768, and the royal cedula of September 10, 1772, directed that the line of defense be established as recommended by Rubí. Despite a great deal of intervening history, the international boundary line between Mexico and the United States follows with few variations the northern limits of New Spain as specified by Rubí. Spain made subsequent advances upon the flanks of her North American possessions, in California, Louisiana, and the Floridas, but not through the Apache barrier.

Three documents stand out in importance among hundreds of others related to the reorganization of New Spain's northern frontiers. The new regulation for presidios which officially established the frontier line is described as follows: *Reglamento e instrucción para los presidios que se han de formar en la linea de frontera de la Nueva España. Resuelto por el Rey N. S. en cedula de*

ix

10 de Septiembre de 1772. This document has been printed, first in Madrid in 1772, and again in Basilio José Arrillaga, *Recopilación de Leyes, Decretos, Bandos, Reglamentos, Circulares y Providencias de los Supremos Poderes de los Estados-Unidos Mexicanos* . . . Vol. IX, pp. 139-187 (Mexico, 1835). There is a contemporary manuscript copy in the Bancroft Library, University of California.

The document which essentially laid the basis for the "new regulation of presidios" was signed at Tacubaya on April 10, 1768, and bears the title, *Digttamen que de orden del Exmo. Señor Marqués de Croix, Virrey de estte Reyno expone el Mariscal de Campo Marqués de Rubí, en orden á la mejor Sittuazion de los Presidios, para la defensa, y exttension de su Frontera á la Genttilidad en los Confines al Nortte de este Virreynatto.* The original is in the Archivo General de Indias, Sevilla, classified under Audiencia de Guadalajara, Legajo 511 (104-6-13), and a copy is in the Archivo General de la Nación, "Historia," Tomo 51, Mexico City. The third document, written by Nicolás Lafora, was fundamental to the preparation of Rubí's recommendations or *dictamen*. Its title is *Relación del Viaje que de orden del excelentíssimo Señor Virrey Marquéz de Cruillas, Hizo el Capitán de Ingenieros Don Nicolás de La Fora en Compañia del Mariscal de Campo Marquéz de Rubí comisionado por Su Magestad. A la Revista de los Presidios internos, zituados en la Frontéra de la parte de la America Septentrional perteneciente al Rey.* The document is the most extensive of the three and in many ways the most interesting. Lafora kept a diary of the inspection tour, wrote descriptions of the areas visited, and made suggestions for the improvement of defenses of the frontier presidios. In his *dictamen*, Rubí acknowledged Lafora's assistance in planning presidial defense reorganization, and the King in the "new regulation of presidios" specified that those on the northern frontier should be located according to the map drawn by Lafora.

One copy of Lafora's diary is in the Biblioteca Nacional, Madrid (No. 5963), and another is in the Biblioteca Nacional, Mexico City. The latter originally contained 100 folios written by a professional scribe, but folios 81 to 88 inclusive are now missing. In Bancroft Library there is a contemporary copy of somewhat more than the first third of the diary. It was this copy which first interested me in Lafora and the Rubí inspection tour.

During a visit to Mexico in 1936 I examined Lafora's diary in the Biblioteca Nacional and learned that the distinguished historian, Don Vito Alessio Robles, had obtained photostatic copies of the manuscript in Madrid which would fill the missing part of the Mexican copy. When I met him, he explained that he was preparing the document for publication. The volume under the title of *Nicolás de Lafora, Relación del Viaje que Hizo a los Presidios Internos* . . . came off the press in 1939. It was carefully edited and contained a reproduction of the map drawn by Lafora of all the frontier regions of New Spain and the presidial locations mentioned in the cedula of September 10, 1772. The original of the map is in the Ministerio del Ejército, Servicio Geográfico, Sección Topografía, Madrid. Miss Inez Haaze, using a photographic enlargement, has redrawn Lafora's map in a more legible form for this volume.

My interest in the three documents mentioned in this preface led to their translation many years ago. Professor George P. Hammond, director of Bancroft Library and managing editor of the Quivira Society, has suggested that the English version of the Lafora diary should be published because of its bearing upon the history of the United States as well as that of Mexico. I thank him for his encouragement and for making available to me a tremendous amount of material related to the subject and obtained from Spanish and Mexican archives through his Bancroft Library microfilming program. At his suggestion I have presented Lafora's report of the Rubí expedition in the broad setting of New Spain's northern borderland history. The central theme is the significance of the presidio as a Spanish frontier institution.

In the preparation of this book I have had expert assistance. Dr. Lucia B. Kinnaird read the entire manuscript before each revision and offered essential advice. Dr. Gwendolyn B. Cobb, a linguist of great competence, carefully checked the translation of Lafora's report and made many improvements. To both I express my gratitude and appreciation. I thank Colonel Manuel G. Baquero y S. de Vicuña of the Spanish Army for his graciousness in taking time from editorial work upon the monumental *Cartografía de Ultramar* to show me Lafora's map and many others of the same area. The initial phases of the work were facilitated by a research grant from the University of California Institute of Social Sciences.

Berkeley, California   LAWRENCE KINNAIRD

CONTENTS

LIST OF PLATES

MAP

The Frontiers of New Spain

Improvement of defenses on New Spain's northern frontiers was an imperative objective in the general Spanish reorganization program following the Seven Years' War. For many years hostile Indian pressure had been increasing and by 1763 it was critical. Across the continent from the Gila valley to the borders of Louisiana, Apaches and other warlike tribes were driving in upon frontier establishments, destroying ranches, running off livestock, and killing settlers. Most dangerous of all Indians in the border regions of the viceroyalty were the Apaches. These were divided into many bands or subtribes which included Gileños, Jicarillos, Carlanes, Chilpaines, Pharaones, Natages, Mescaleros, and Lipanes. Pushing in upon the eastern Apaches and driving them to the south and west were mounted and mobile bands of Comanches. In many places the Spanish frontier had actually receded. New Mexico had become an outpost, an island of settlement in a sea of Apaches, Comanches, and other northern tribes. In Sonora the Pimas had recently rebelled and the Seris were unpacified. Losses inflicted by raiding Indians upon Spanish frontier establishments amounted annually to hundreds of lives and thousands of head of livestock.

Seeking a solution to frontier problems, Charles III commissioned the Marqués de Rubí to inspect all presidios in the viceroyalty of New Spain and to recommend measures for improvement. Rubí, with the rank of field marshal and the titles of commander in the order of Alcántara, and Baron of Llinas, was a man of great influence in both military and political circles of Spain. His full name was Cayetano María Pignatelli Rubí Corbera y San Climent, and his parents were Francisco Pignatelli, lieutenant general of the Kingdom of Aragon and ambassador to France, and María Francisca Rubí Corbera y San Climent, second Marquesa de Rubí and Baroness of Llinas. With this background and array of titles, his opinions and recommendations carried much weight.

While the King gave the responsibility for overhauling the military organization of the frontier provinces to Rubí, he dispatched José de Gálvez to New Spain with the title of *visitador general* and authority to institute sweeping reforms in the administrative and financial functions of the viceroyalty. The missions of these two distinguished men were independent, each performing his special assignment in the reform program. Rubí's task was not unique in the history of the viceroyalty. Pedro de Rivera in the years 1724-1728 made an extensive inspection tour of the northern frontiers and recommended many reforms and improvements in the military establishments. Yet forty years later, as Rubí began his inspection, conditions were no better than they had been in Rivera's time.

The best account of Rubí's tour of inspection was written by Nicolás de Lafora, Captain of the Spanish Royal Engineers. Viceroy Cruillas assigned him to duty with the field marshal's party for the purpose of mapping and describing accurately the regions visited. The engineer's report contains a day-by-day narrative of the journey which lasted twenty-three months and covered, according to his estimate, 2,936 Spanish leagues or more than 7,600 miles. Included in the report are descriptions of the provinces of Nueva Vizcaya, New Mexico, Sonora, Coahuila, Texas, Nueva Galicia, and Nayarit.[1]

1. The best account of Lafora's career is published in Vito Alessio Robles, *Nicolás de Lafora, Relación del Viaje que Hizo a los Presidios Internos Situados en la Frontera de la America Septentrional Perteneciente al Rey de España* (Mexico, D.F., 1939).

In the preparation of his report, Lafora used documents obtained from governmental archives in Mexico and from the presidios visited in the course of his tour with the Marqués de Rubí. Frontier officials and local guides or escorts pointed out geographical features en route. A prodigious amount of detail is contained in the report. Even the most insignificant settlements and the smallest arroyos are specifically named. Meticulous information is given about geographical features, population statistics, and frontier conditions. His knowledge of Indians in the borderlands was also extensive. Practically every tribe known to modern anthropologists and many others whose history is still obscure are mentioned. Everywhere along the northern frontier he heard stories about the savage Apaches and their audacious exploits—how they raided ranches and even immobilized whole presidial garrisons by stampeding their horses. He concluded his report by recommending improvement in methods of warfare against the Apaches.

In addition to keeping a record of the Rubí expedition, Lafora produced a manuscript which, for its time, is the best single source of information upon the frontiers of New Spain yet found.

Although the Marqués de Rubí received his commission directly from the King and was responsible to him through Julián de Arriaga, Minister of the Indies, he was informed that the viceroy would give him his instructions. Arriving in Mexico City in the middle of December, he expected to organize his expedition, receive his instructions, and depart for the North. Irked by the delay which followed, for he was not a man of exceptional patience, he wrote to Viceroy Cruillas on February 17, 1766:

Summoned by Your Excellency under date of December 7th last, I arrived at this capital on the 17th of the same month where, within a short time (so your Excellency said) you would be able to instruct me regarding the changes up to that time in new regulations for presidios. . . . And now having already spent more than two months without receiving instructions, I am regretfully and inevitably compelled to beg Your Excellency to indicate the exact time which you consider advisable for my departure so that the failure to comply with the order of the King for so long a time may not be imputed by my negligence, and also because the maintenance of the horses and the necessary servants, who are fed at his expense, has already become insupportable to me since it is making the journey impossible even before it is begun. Therefore, I shall be compelled to release both the horses and servants until the exact time Your Excellency sees fit to arrange for my departure.[2]

The viceroy excused the delay on the ground that much time had been spent in assembling from various government offices all the documents which might be useful to Rubí during his tour of inspection. An additional explanation was that Joseph Urrutia, Ensign of the Regiment of America, had been assigned to the expedition as cartographer, and he needed time for preparing and packing materials and instruments he would require for the journey.[3] The marqués completed his own preparations, arranged his finances, and notified Cruillas that he planned to depart on March 10 regardless of Urrutia's readiness to travel.

On the date set for departure, Rubí finally received his instructions together with documents and maps for his guidance. A receipt signed by him on March 10, 1766, listed the following items:

1. A report by the Auditor of War, containing the enumeration, names and description, location, and history of each and every

2. Rubí to Cruillas, Mexico, February 17, 1766, Archivo General de Indias, Audiencia de Guadalajara, 103-4-15 [273]. All archival materials used are from the great microfilm collection of Bancroft Library, University of California. Recent classification numbers are indicated in brackets.

3. Cruillas to Rubí, Mexico, February 20, 1766, A.G.I., Aud. de Guadalajara, 103-4-15 [273].

one of the presidios, with statement of the officers, men, and equipment of the same.

2. A map of the provinces of Nueva Vizcaya, New Mexico, Sonora, Sinaloa, Nuevo Reyno de León, Coahuila, Texas, the Californias, Nuevo Santander, on which is also shown the exact location of presidios, their names, the names of their captains, number of men, and amount of their allotments.

3. A special map (the most accurate one), showing only the boundaries and location of the provinces of Sonora and Sinaloa.

4. An accurate map of the New Kingdom of Toledo (including the Province of San Joseph de Nayarit) showing the boundaries of New Galicia.

5. Another topographical map, made by the engineer who accompanied Brigadier Don Pedro Rivera, covering the provinces of Nueva Vizcaya, part of New Mexico, part of Nayarit, part of Sonora, of Ostimuri, Sinaloa, and Culiacán, under the general name of Nueva Galicia, indicating separately the rancherías of pacified Indians and those of savage tribes.[4]

The collection of maps turned over to Rubí had a bearing upon the nature of the general map later drawn by Lafora in view of the fact that it contained a great amount of information and detail which could not have been acquired through observations made during the journey. Like most maps it was a composite with new data added.

The viceroy's instructions contained the general plan for the inspection tour and named most of the presidios that Rubí should visit. Cruillas emphasized the importance of Sonora, and, without mentioning any presidios specifically, suggested the advisability of some relocations. Rubí was relieved of responsibility for one section of his instructions pertaining to Sonora. He had been directed to investigate the possibility of transporting supplies to the presidios and

4. Receipt signed by Rubí, Mexico, March 10, 1766, A.G.I., Aud. de Guadalajara, 103-4-15 [273].

mines of the northern frontier by small ships which might sail from Acapulco into the Gila river via the Gulf of California and the Colorado river. José de Gálvez, the *visitador general,* took over this investigation. Despite his somewhat limited geographical knowledge, Cruillas covered the Texas situation briefly but thoroughly. He directed Rubí to consider the advisability of changing the location of San Sabá on the west and, in view of Spanish acquisition of Louisiana, of abandoning the establishments of eastern Texas. The viceroy concluded his instructions with the general statement:

"The Señor Marqués shall ascertain what should be done in each province and presidio, and it will be advisable for him always to accompany his reports by a small map, even though it be a simple sketch by the engineer, in order to show better the country in question, noting for clarity the boundaries and principal routes."[5]

Revealing his great interest in the whole project, Cruillas ordered that "the Marqués de Rubí should promptly advise the viceroyship of the province and place where he is, what occurred there, the place where he will go next, and the measures he requires, requests and considers advisable." In case urgent matters should arise during the inspection, Rubí was authorized to send reports to the capital by special courier at the expense of the royal treasury.

Rubí's itinerary was divided geographically into three phases—inspection of the regions on the route to Santa Fé, the western tour through Sonora, and the long journey to eastern Texas. Both going and returning, the field marshal wherever possible traversed different routes. Immediately after receiving his instructions, he and the main portion

5. Instructions of Cruillas to Rubí, Mexico, March 10, 1766, A.G.I., Aud. de Guadalajara, 103-4-15 [273].

of his party left Mexico City for Durango, capital of Nueva Vizcaya, where they arrived on April 11, 1766. Lafora departed from Mexico on March 18 and joined Rubí in Durango on April 14. Lafora's route lay through Querétaro, Celaya, Salamanca, Silao, León, Aguascalientes, Zacatecas, Fresnillo, and Sombrerete and approximately followed the modern Mexican Highway No. 45. The chief business in Durango was an inquiry into the delay in establishing two new presidios authorized for Nueva Vizcaya by the Council of War held on October 9, 1765. The governor, Don Joseph Carlos de Agüero, did not entirely satisfy the field marshal with his explanations.[6] After some difficulty in securing additional pack animals, the inspection party left Durango on April 26.

On the last day of April, Rubí reached El Pasaje, the first of the presidios named in the viceroy's instructions. He proceeded with a routine of inspection which, with slight variations, he used at all presidios visited. Immediately upon arrival, the field marshal inspected the garrison and the horses. He found that most of the men and mounts were of superior quality. Administration and equipment were another story. Carelessness and irregularity existed in matters of soldiers' pay and charges made to them for clothing and other necessities. Consequently, Rubí took statements from individual soldiers concerning methods of adjusting their pay, prices charged them for provisions and rations, tasks imposed upon them other than drill, improper deductions from their pay, and inequality in the service. He discovered that accounts were adjusted without the soldiers knowing whether prices charged them were higher than specified in the Regulations. The next step in the inspection was to audit the books of the presidial commander, Captain Bernardo de Vargas Zevallos. Rubí

6. Rubí to Cruillas, Durango, April 15, 1766, A.G.I., Aud. de Guadalajara, 103-4-15 [273].

gave orders for correction of abuses and directed that booklets should be given to each soldier in which he should enter all items that he purchased and the price. These individual records must agree with the captain's accounts. Armament of the presidio was not in much better condition than the captain's books. Guns were of different calibers, swords were of poor quality, and there was a shortage of lances. Shields and uniforms were of many designs, and most of the leather jackets needed repair. The amount of powder allotted to each soldier was inadequate for active service.[7]

Rubí spent two weeks inspecting El Pasaje, and during the same period Lafora was engaged in mapping the area. As the marshal was departing, he admonished the commander to be more active in the defense of the province against raiding Apaches.

On the road northward from El Pasaje, Rubí's party passed El Gallo and Cerro Gordo, where the walls of old presidios had fallen into decay. Cerro Gordo, now Villa Hidalgo, had been founded in 1648. Despite withdrawal of presidial garrisons, small villages remained at the sites. Before reaching Guajoquilla, Rubí traversed the fertile and well-watered San Bartolomé valley, in which several prosperous haciendas were located. The town of San Bartolomé had a thriving population of 4,751 Spaniards, mestizos, and mulattoes. The mulattoes were probably descendants of slaves brought in to work the mines during the previous century. The pueblo of Las Bocas, exclusively inhabited by Tarahumares Indians, was located nearby. The San Bartolomé valley, for Rubí and his party, was the beginning of the frontier. It was the first place encountered subject to Indian raids, and near it also was Atotonilco, the

7. Rubí to Cruillas, El Pasaje, May 11, 12, and 13, 1766, A.G.I., Aud. de Guadalajara, 103-4-15 [273].

first mission they had seen. Situated on the Florido river, the mission had a population of three hundred Tarahumares Indians and was supervised by a Franciscan. Today, Villa López is located at this place, and a short distance farther north is Jiménez which was the site of the old presidio of Guajoquilla.

Rubí's inspection of the presidio of Nuestra Señora de las Caldas de Guajoquilla followed the procedure used at El Pasaje and required thirteen days. The viceroy had directed that the marqués should ascertain whether its present location was satisfactory for the defense of Nueva Vizcaya "from savage Indians and to prevent the frequent outrages which they have committed on the Camino Real, the cattle and haciendas which they are said to have destroyed atrociously since the abandonment of the presidios of Conchos, Cerro Gordo, Gallo, and Mapimí." Guajoquilla was the first presidio to be inspected of those established by Viceroy Revillagigedo in 1752. In that year many Indian outbreaks had occurred on the northern frontier and conditions were unusually serious. Normally the mobile or flying company stationed here numbered sixty-six officers and men. However, the lieutenant and twenty-five men had been detached early in 1766 to create a new presidio in San Buenaventura valley.

The journey to Chihuahua from Guajoquilla required six days and was fraught with some risk because Apaches harassed the region which Rubí's party was now entering. En route they passed the abandoned presidio of Conchos located on the banks of the river of that name. Where the presidio had once been there was the small pueblo of Guadalupe in which twenty-five poverty-stricken Spaniards lived. Approximately thirty miles beyond Guadalupe were the ruins of Chancaple, the first of many settlements seen by Rubí which had been deserted as a result of Indian attacks. Beyond Chancaple, travelers were in great danger from Apache raiders.

San Phelipe el Real de Chihuahua contained a mixed population of four hundred families and was in deplorable condition. Once a rich mining town, now it had no means of subsistence. For the most part, its gold and silver mines were deserted because to operate them was to risk torture and death at the hands of the barbarous Apaches. The Chihuahua region was typical of many northern frontier settlements. Spaniards, mestizos, and mulattoes composed the population. In adjacent pueblos and missions docile Indians were undergoing the process of Hispanization. Amalgamation of these heterogeneous elements was being hastened by pressure from outlying savage tribes because this situation forced coöperation in the common effort for defense and survival. For the Spaniards, with the exception of the great hacendados, frontier life was a return to the primitive and to poverty. Existence was precarious from every aspect. Some great fortunes had been made in mining, but others had been lost. Many prospectors and miners earned only a bare living. There were a few cattle barons, but they were usually not found on the most dangerous frontiers. Small ranchers and herders were at the mercy of Apache parasites who emerged from their mountain and desert retreats to drive off livestock in surprise forays.

For the harassed frontiersmen, a town—even a poor one like Chihuahua—became a refuge from enemy Indians. Incursions from the Natage country and the Sierra de Santa Rosa had destroyed the properous haciendas of Hormigas, San Bernardo, Agua Nueva, El Alamo, Chorreras, and Bachiniva. Even those at Tabalaopa and Mula, adjacent to the town of Chihuahua, had been ruined. The area under attack extended beyond Lake Parras and into the interior of Nueva Vizcaya. For many years the

Camino Real to Durango had been unsafe for travel. Towns, such as Chihuahua and Durango, had developed usually as supply centers in regions of active mining and ranching operations. People engaged in commerce or transportation of supplies congregated in these towns. In times of danger refugees from mines and ranches were added to the population. Despite their haphazard growth, towns marked a more permanent frontier advance than missions or presidios.

Rubí and Lafora remained at Chihuahua for twenty-five days studying the area and drawing up recommendations for improved defense. The completed plan, together with a map drawn by Lafora, was dispatched to the viceroy on July 5, 1766.[8] During Rubí's stay in Chihuahua, Ensign Juan Baptista del Peru, on detached service from Guajoquilla, was assigned to duty with him. This officer assisted the marqués in restocking provisions and served as his escort to El Paso.

Peru had an interesting background. With some companions he had come to New Mexico from French Canada in 1750. At Santa Fé he became acquainted with Captain Fernando de Bustamante Tagle who befriended him; and, when this officer was transferred to Nueva Vizcaya, Peru followed him and enlisted in the Spanish military service. His competence and enterprise earned him the rank of ensign. Peru favorably impressed Rubí, who had a keen appreciation of military talent. An investigation of Peru's record revealed that he was a brave and intelligent officer. The field marshal recommended that the viceroy promote him to the command of a *volante,* or flying company, which would be constantly employed in following

8. Lafora made an extensive report upon the defense problems of Nueva Vizcaya and offered recommendations for improvement. *Dictamen* of Nicolás de Lafora, San Phelipe Real de Chihuahua, July 5, 1766, A.G.I., Aud. de Guadalajara, 104-6-13 [511].

the trails and punishing Indians who harassed the vicinity of Chihuahua.[9]

The next presidial garrison which Rubí planned to inspect was, according to his information, stationed at the confluence of the Conchos and Río Grande rivers and known as La Junta. Leaving Chihuahua on July 7, the inspection party passed Chinarras, a Jesuit mission for the Conchos Indians; Santa Ana, which had once been a Jesuit mission; and San Gerónimo, a Franciscan mission for the Tarahumares. Beyond these was the Hacienda Palo Blanco, abandoned because of enemy Apaches. After three days' travel, by chance Rubí met a party which gave him news that the captain of the presidio of La Junta de los Ríos had abandoned the place by order of Governor Joseph de Agüero. The informants stated that the garrison was already three days on the march to the town of Julimes, the new location of the presidio. Neither the governor nor the captain of the garrison had informed Rubí of any such plan. From the deserted hacienda of Hormigas, on July 10, 1766, he reported his displeasure to the viceroy and explained that he could not, under the circumstances, inspect a garrison which was then on the march. Since it was not practical to order the troops to return to La Junta de los Ríos and it was impossible to reach Julimes because the Conchos river was in flood and could not be forded, he notified the viceroy that he would go directly to El Paso and thence to New Mexico. Rubí made it clear, however, that he believed the decision to move the presidial garrison to Julimes was unwise. In his opinion, a presidio at the junction of the Conchos and Río Grande would be far more effective in defending the frontier against Apache incursions from the north.

9. Statement by Fernando de Bustamante Tagle, August 26, 1766; Rubí to Cruillas, July 27, 1766; Peru to Croix, August 8, 1766, A.G.I., Aud. de Guadalajara, 103-4-15 [273].

The remainder of the journey to El Paso was through a devastated region. Three days beyond the abandoned hacienda of Hormigas the party arrived at the hacienda of Agua Nueva. There a few servants had been able to survive because the establishment was surrounded by an adobe wall with circular towers where sentinels were always posted. An outlying flour mill had been abandoned because it was exposed to easy attack, and the proprietor of the hacienda had departed for a safer place. Many of the large landowners on the frontier lived in towns and left the dangerous business of operating their properties to servants. Four leagues beyond Agua Nueva the expedition came upon the main road which ran from Chihuahua through Encinillas to El Paso. At Ojo Caliente it passed another hacienda, once wealthy but now in ruins. Beyond this spot lay the jurisdiction of New Mexico. One hundred and thirty-two days after his departure from Mexico City, the Marqués de Rubí arrived at the presidio of Nuestra Señora del Pilar del Paso del Río del Norte.

As a result of the New Mexico Pueblo revolt of 1680, the establishment at El Paso had become important. In that bloody uprising the Pueblo Indians slaughtered 400 Spaniards, including twenty-one Franciscan missionaries. A surviving Spanish population of about 2,200 fled southward to the El Paso region. Failure by Governor Otermín to reconquer New Mexico in 1681 led to the permanent settlement of El Paso and the construction of a presidio in 1683. Franciscans were successful in their work among the Indians of the area, and several missions were erected along the river as far as La Junta where the Conchos flowed into the Río Grande. This activity, however, was in the face of spreading Indian resistance. A series of Indian uprisings all along the frontier followed that of New Mexico. To strength northern defenses, a number of presidios were established: El Pasaje, El Gallo, and Conchos in

1685; Monclova in 1687; Casas Grandes and Janos in 1690; and Fronteras in 1695. A rebellion, second in importance only to that of New Mexico, occurred in 1690 among the Tarahumares of Nueva Vizcaya and threatened to isolate the El Paso settlement. Strenuous efforts by combined forces from many presidios eventually crushed the uprising and opened the way for another attempt to reconquer New Mexico. Diego Vargas Zapata Luján Ponce de León was appointed governor in 1692 especially for this purpose. Assembling his forces at El Paso, he began a series of campaigns against the Pueblo Indians. The reconquest was, however, not completed until 1697, a year after Vargas had been succeeded as governor by Cubero. In the interval El Paso had become a way station and supply depot for the invading forces. Although separated from the re-established New Mexico by a wide expanse of wild country, El Paso at the time of Rubí's visit was still within the jurisdiction of New Mexico, the capital of which was Santa Fé.

El Paso and environs had a larger population than any other place visited by Rubí after leaving Durango. Along the right bank of the Río Grande within a distance of less than twenty miles there were five pueblos and the hacienda of Los Tiburcios. The pueblo of San Lorenzo del Río was inhabited by Sumas Indians, San Antonio de Senecú by Piros, San Antonio de la Isleta by Tiguas, and La Purísima Concepción del Socorro by more Piros. Spaniards and mestizos made up the population of the hacienda and a part of each pueblo. The agriculture of the region was flourishing and Lafora noted that there was a surplus of many European fruits. Grapes were as good as those of Spain. Wine was fair and brandy better. Because of El Paso's economic stability and its population of at least 5,000, Rubí believed that it could defend itself through the organization of competent militia under a responsible chief.

In his opinion the garrison would contribute more to the defense of the frontier if moved back to Carrizal and placed under the jurisdiction of Nueva Vizcaya.

Departing from El Paso on August 5, Rubí began the journey to Santa Fé, which he estimated as 135 Spanish leagues. A short distance from the town, the party crossed the Río Grande on rafts and traveled thereafter on the river's eastern side. Beyond the crossing lay a 250-mile stretch of country, uninhabited save by roving Apache bands. Within this distance was the notorious Jornada del Muerto, completely waterless most of the year. Nevertheless, the road on the east side of the river was preferable to the route along the west bank because it was shorter and passed through more open country where travelers were less liable to Apache ambush. Despite that fact, when the party camped at a place named Perilla, on the night of August 9, Apaches attempted to steal the horses. Discovered by a sentry, they were driven off. The following day they attacked a party of Sumas Indians who were driving a flock of sheep for Rubí's party. They stole the animals, but most of them were recovered by a mounted detachment which Rubí sent in pursuit. The Apaches, however, were persistent. They followed the expedition throughout the day but were careful to keep out of musket range.

As the party entered New Mexico, after a 200-mile journey from El Paso, it came upon reminders of the great Pueblo revolt eighty-six years previous. Among these were the ruins of the houses of Luis López and Felipe Romero and those of the pueblos of Socorro and Alamillo. Additional evidences of havoc were scattered along the route to the north. A struggling new settlement named Las Nutrias had recently been planted in the area and, because it was the southernmost outpost of New Mexico proper, the inhabitants were constantly menaced by Apaches. From here to the north, pueblos and missions were distributed in increasing numbers along the line of travel and also on the other side of the Río Grande. Passing through the Villa of Albuquerque, Rubí hastened on to Santa Fé, capital of the province. He remained here twenty-seven days carrying out his inspection and discussing frontier problems with Governor Tomás Vélez Cachupin. New Mexico's isolation was obvious, and Rubí's plan to remove the garrison of regular troops from El Paso would make the situation worse. The commander of that presidio had supplied guards for caravans traveling the precarious route to Santa Fé, but a local militia could not be expected to do so.

Rubí therefore proposed a scheme which he hoped would keep open the line of communication between El Paso and the New Mexican establishments. He recommended that a new settlement should be made at a site named Robledo located on the Río Grande about twenty leagues north of El Paso. He outlined his plan as follows:

Even without increasing the number of presidios, in order to avoid the risk that their permanency should be insisted upon by interested parties on account of the value of their allotments, there could be established here a settlement, drawn from El Paso del Norte, of those unfortunate people who have little or no part in the distribution of the lands of that highly populated area. In the beginning this settlement should be protected by a detachment of thirty men and one officer from the Presidio of Santa Fé. These in my opinion, can be taken from that troop and reinforced with thirty auxiliaries made up of citizens of any character or color. To these, for the obligatory and fixed term of ten years, may be assigned fifteen pesos monthly in coin each.[10]

The field marshal hoped that at the end of ten years the settlement would be self-sustaining and an effective barrier

10. Rubí's *dictamen*, Tacubaya, April 10, 1768, A.G.I., Aud. de Guadalajara, 104-6-13 [511].

against the Natage and Gila Apaches. A much longer time elapsed before such an outpost was planted at Robledo. Fifteen years after Rubí had visited the place, the first *comandante general* of the Interior Provinces, Teodoro de Croix, reported to José de Gálvez that "having reconnoitered the spot of Robledo, and finding no suitable place to establish the detachment . . . Lieutenant Colonel Don Juan Bautista de Anza agreed with the opinion of his predecessor and proposed to me that the forces destined for Robledo be established at the abandoned pueblo of Socorro."[11] Yet, militarily, Rubí may have been correct in his selection of a location. If the place he had in mind was across the Río Grande from Mount Robledo, it was the same site the United States Army chose upon which to build Fort Selden in 1865, during Apache outbreaks. Fort Selden and Fort Bliss near El Paso contributed much to the elimination of hostile Apaches from the region, but this was a century after Rubí's time.

As he was departing from Santa Fé the field marshal received news that the Marqués de Croix had succeeded Cruillas as viceroy. The return journey to El Paso was accomplished in thirteen days, and from that place Rubí wrote to the new viceroy on October 7, 1766, concerning the progress of his work and his plans:

I call Your Excellency's attention to the order of the King under which I am making an inspection of all the presidios of this Kingdom. In their execution and continuation I shall proceed from here through those of San Buenaventura, Janos, and Sonora to the presidio of San Miguel de Horcacitas. I have forwarded the summaries and documents covering the inspections which I have made of the companies at Pasaje and Hauxoquilla in Nueva Vizcaya and acknowledgement of their receipt by the Marqués de Cruillas who also advises me of receipt of a project signed by the Captain of Engineers,

11. Alfred Barnaby Thomas, *Teodoro de Croix and the Northern Frontier of New Spain, 1776-1783* (Norman, Okla., 1941), pp. 106-107.

Don Nicolás de Lafora, for the repair and better defense of the said province. . . .[12]

From El Paso, Rubí retraced the road through Carrizal to Ojo Caliente, where he planned to begin his western tour of inspection. Near the latter place was the fortified hacienda of El Carmen, whose owner employed or supported 291 persons. He maintained thirty-five men at arms as guards, most of whom were Spaniards. El Carmen suffered losses of livestock, but was too strong for Apaches to destroy. Haciendas of this type were feudal in character and usually were created by large grants of land made to members of Spanish or creole aristocracy.

The inspection group turned west from Ojo Caliente to San Buenaventura located in a valley of the same name. The trail was hazardous all the way, and the field marshal took the precaution of sending out a reconnoitering party before entering the most dangerous defile. In the valley itself, habitations were scattered along a distance of about five miles. The garrison was composed of fifty-one soldiers and forty local militiamen. In the pueblo where the soldiers lived, the houses formed an enclosure, but there was no other fortification. Twelve days were spent inspecting this area. Evidence of Apache raids was everywhere present. A short distance to the northwest was a ruined hacienda, and throughout the area a great deal of farm land was abandoned. Rubí's comments upon the location of the presidio were caustic:

The Presidio of San Buenaventura was newly erected in the valley of this name with little premeditated foresight by the governor of Nueva Vizcaya. Although entrusted with this task, he delegated it to Captain Don Manuel de Villaverde who, being little versed in such matters, located it in a position so advantageous for

12. Rubí to Croix, El Paso del Río del Norte, October 7, 1766, A.G.I., Aud. de Guadalajara, 103-4-15 [273].

the enemy that they themselves could not have suggested anything better for the total destruction and extermination of this presidio. . . . It is exposed to innumerable hidden approaches through which the enemy has penetrated here. Both in former times and recently, the enemies have committed the most bloody atrocities, including the killing of Captain Campillo of Vizcaya, and innumerable officers, soldiers, and inhabitants of this settlement.[13]

Although the purpose of the presidio was to protect Chihuahua and its dependent haciendas and pueblos, its location in the inaccessible Sierra de San Miguel rendered it useless. Rubí believed that the presidio of San Buenaventura could check Apache incursions from the north much better if it were located in the valley of Ruíz near Laguna de Ascensión and southeast of the Laguna de Guzmán.

From San Buenaventura the inspection party set out for the presidio of Janos, passing Las Casas Grandes de Moctezuma. Here ancient ruins were flanked by ruins of modern houses whose inhabitants had perished at Apaches' hands. Travel through the mountains by a rough road to Janos was perilous at all times, and the most dangerous place was Ramos pass where the trail was lined with crosses over the graves of people who had been killed by Apaches. Inspection of Presidio San Felipe y Santiago de Janos required fifteen days. Rubí was favorably impressed by the location:

The old Presidio of Janos (belonging to Nueva Vizcaya) is the one nearest to the Province of Gila and the rancherías scattered along the banks of the Gila, San Francisco and Las Mimbres rivers. . . . This presidio is considered the best situated of all those in this locality because of its ability to reconnoiter quickly the passes most frequented by the Gileños and to aid its neighbors Fronteras and San Buenaventura.[14]

13. Rubí's *dictamen,* April 10, 1768, A.G.I., Aud. de Guadalajara, 104-6-13 [511].
14. *Ibid.*

Other conditions at Janos, however, were miserable. The population consisted of 101 families of mestizos and mulattoes and totaled 455 persons including the fifty-one men of the garrison. Most of the people had no means of subsistence, and their houses were disintegrating.

After fifteen days the inspection group proceeded to the Presidio of Corodeguachi or Fronteras, in the jurisdiction of Sonora. Most of the five-day journey lay through uninhabited mountainous regions or lands abandoned because of Apaches. After a sixteen-day inspection of Fronteras, and the surrounding area, Rubí decided that the presidio's location was poor. The distance of sixty leagues from Janos was too great for military coöperation. He considered forty leagues the best interval between presidios and proposed that the garrison be moved to the valley of San Bernardo.

The next presidio on Rubí's itinerary was Terrenate. On the road his party passed the sites of at least four pueblos deserted because of Apaches. The presidio, which bore the official name of San Felipe de Jesús Guebabi, had a population of only 300, including the soldiers stationed there. Climate was bad and land so poor that settlers planted their crops in the Sobaípuris valley, five leagues away, despite the fact that their storehouse there had been burned two or three times. The field marshal decided that the site of Terrenate should also be changed.

Its location, considered only with regard to its own defense, may be called good, in view of the character of the enemies. However, as this point is considered the least important advantage of a presidio, whose most remote risk is that of being besieged, we must seek the more important one of preventing the passage of the enemies together with that of all possible proximity [to other presidios] in order to receive the assistance needed on various occasions.[15]

15. *Ibid.*

To the west of Terrenate, Rubí and party entered the Jesuit mission field of Pimería Alta, but the story of Apache depredations was the same. Everywhere were vacant ranches whose owners had fled or had been less fortunate. The missions fared better. They passed Mission Santa María Suamca and Mission Guebabi, both inhabited by Upper Pimas and formerly administered by Jesuits. Tumacácori, an old Jesuit mission, was now a Pápago pueblo. Under the leadership of Father Eusebio Kino, the Jesuits had entered Sonora in 1687. Mission Dolores in the upper Sonora valley became the headquarters for Jesuit activities among the Upper Pimas between Altar and the Gila river. Kino founded Mission San Xavier del Bac in 1700, and shortly thereafter, Guebabi and Tumacácori, all in the Santa Cruz valley. Their locations helped to define the northern limits of New Spain.

The period following the death of Kino in 1711 was one of decline for the Sonora missions, largely due to a lack of governmental support. A visit to the area by the Bishop of Durango in 1725, and the inspection tour of Pedro de Rivera which began the following year, led to renewed government interest. Additional missionaries were sent to Sonora in 1732, and formerly abandoned northern missions were reoccupied. Orderly development of missions, however, was disturbed by opening of mines in the upper Altar valley. Discovery at Arizonac of silver nuggets of amazing size led to a mining rush. Although the mines were depleted within a few years, from the Jesuits' point of view the damage had been done. They recognized that the usual cycle of developments upon a missionary frontier was under way. Peaceful mission operation was followed in turn by intrusion of ranchers and miners, Indian resistance to encroachment and bad treatment, general uprisings, crushing of rebellion by military force, establishment of presidios, arrival of new settlers, and eventual demands for secularization.

Coincidental with the Altar valley mining boom, Indian troubles arose both in Sonora and Sinaloa. To protect the increasing Spanish population and hold the Indians in check, new presidios were founded in 1741 at Pitiqui, not far from Caborca, and at Terrenate. Indian hostilities increased and by 1750 a general war had developed with the Seris. Revillagigedo, who was then viceroy, ordered Diego Parrilla, the governor of Sonora, to carry on a campaign of extermination against them. However, war against the Seris was complicated in 1751 by a general uprising among the northern Pimas. Along the northern frontier more than a hundred persons lost their lives, including the Jesuits at Caborca and Sonóita. Mines, ranches, and missions were abandoned. Parrilla was successful in suppressing the Pima rebellion, but intermittent hostilities by the Seris continued. Rubí, whose visit to Sonora was fifteen years later, found that the Seris were still a menace. Most of the missions had been reopened, but, in regions adjacent to the Seris, many mines and ranches were too exposed to be operated.

In Sonora the Pima revolt forced the advance of the presidial frontier as other Indian uprisings had done elsewhere. Revillagigedo ordered the establishment of presidios at Altar, not far from Caborca, and Tubac, south of San Xavier del Bac. Mission importance was somewhat reduced by expansion of the presidial frontier and many disagreements over jurisdiction and authority occurred between missionaries and military officials. In fact, such disputes between church and state constituted a common characteristic of all Spanish frontiers. Despite animosity of the military toward the Jesuits, there is no evidence that the Marqués de Rubí, at the time of his inspection of Sonora in 1767, had any knowledge that Jesuit expulsion from all Spanish possessions was to take place during that year. The mission system in general had been a less costly method of establishing control over the Indian population of northern Mexico than military force, but the latter was always needed in time of crisis. The presidio as a Spanish frontier institution was as important as the mission. Presidios became, in many instances, nuclei of frontier towns. In outlying districts, despite danger, hardship, and poverty, small settlements of Spaniards, Hispanized Indians, and a mixture of both elements grew up under protection of presidial garrisons. As settlers moved in, presidios tended to supersede the missions, but the presidial frontier seldom advanced beyond that of the mission. Upon reaching the Apache country both missionary and soldier were stalemated. To study the presidial frontier involved in the Apache dilemma was precisely Rubí's assignment.

The inspection party spent Christmas and New Year's Day at San Ignacio de Tubac, the northernmost Sonoran presidio. The personality and intelligence of its commander, Captain Juan Bautista de Anza, impressed the field marshal and he commended him officially for his honesty and efficiency. Anza's accounts were in excellent condition, and his men asserted that he had not only treated them fairly but also liberally. Under a system where commanding officers customarily profiteered at the expense of their men, this was indeed unusual. Because of Anza's reputation as a just administrator, many settlers had come to Tubac. Rubí believed that Tubac had a large enough population to protect itself and that the garrison should therefore be moved to a location somewhat to the southwest. According to the field marshal, the move would be inexpensive:

Tubac has no inclosure or fortifications at present nor was it allotted any funds for this purpose . . . at the time of its establishment because of uncertainty as to its permanency. For this reason there can be no objection to its removal because the loss or duplication of expense would be only what the captain and soldiers may have expended in the construction of their quarters. . . .

We should consider as the frontier enemies of this presidio these Pápagos or Piattos to the northwest and other less known tribes to the north in the vicinity of the Colorado river. . . . This presidio is also attacked (one raid having occurred while I was inspecting it) by the Apaches of the Western Part (let us so call them) of the Sierra de Gila. These natives are divided into clans like Arabs, and congregate in rancherías or migratory bivouacs and are accustomed to sow and reap their harvests of *mescales* while encamped on some of the plains in the vicinity. From there they make all the raids which are to be most feared by our arms. . . . All the districts of the government of Sonora, as far as Tarahumara, demand of this presidio the greatest vigilance and activity on the part of its commander in reconnoitering, with all frequency possible, the intervening distance between the two posts to the right and left.[16]

A four-day journey took the field marshal and his party to Santa Gertrudis del Altar, the westernmost presidio. On the way they passed the Jesuit missions of Sariqui, Tubutama, and Oquilva. At Altar the problem of defense shifted from Apaches to Seris and Pápagos. Rubí recommended that the presidio be moved to a location southwest of the Jesuit mission of Caborca and adjacent to the Gulf of California. Selection of the site should be made, he said, "after proper surveys of the terrain to make sure of two indispenable requisites, water and pasture for the mounts." The field marshal explained the reason for his recommendation:

The principal object and purpose of this presidio should be the prevention of the invasions or at least the retreats of the Pápago or Piatto Indians, living to the northwest, whose present good relations

16. Rubí's *dictamen*, April 10, 1768, A.G.I., Aud. de Guadalajara, 104-6-13 [511].

with the Seris of the Cerro Prieto make their intercourse most unfortunate, but now difficult to prevent because of the extent, aridity, and roughness of the country where they meet.[17]

Like many other Spanish officers, Rubí expressed the hope that the Seris might be exterminated.

After leaving Altar, and traveling to the south and east, the expedition made its next objective the presidio of San Miguel de Horcasitas. The journey required a week. Along the way there was much evidence of devastation caused by Seris. First was the abandoned ranch of Ocuca and next the ruined Santa Ana ranch. In San Lorenzo pueblo only the sites of houses burned by Seris ten years previously remained. Next was the abandoned rancho Sásabe. Gold placers at the mouth of the Saracache river were deserted because of Apache raids, and other mining and smelting activities along the way were at a standstill. The most thriving establishments on the route were the Opata missions Cucurpe and Opodepe operated by Jesuits. Lafora reported that the worst road in all Sonora was encountered between Opodepe and Horcasitas.

The presidio of Horcasitas was a small and insignificant place despite the fact that, at the time, it was the capital of the province of Sonora and residence of the governor. The officers and men of the presidial company numbered fifty-one, which was the same as in the other Sonora presidios. In addition, there were about sixty civilians and a number of Indian families employed chiefly as servants. Rubí remained in this unimpressive capital for twenty-four days.

Buenavista on the north bank of the Yaqui river was the next presidio to be inspected. In the eight-day journey the expedition passed the Jesuit missions of Ures, Tecoripa, and Comuripa and arrived at the presidio on March 3,

17. *Ibid.*

1767. Southernmost of the Sonora posts, it was located in an area where Jesuit missions had been in operation for more than a century. Fathers Pérez and Pérez de Ribas had founded missions among the Yaquis in 1617 and within a few years there were missions in the upper Yaqui valley. The Ures mission in the Sonora valley was founded in 1636, and by 1650 there were missions at Cucurpe and Arispe. Lafora commented that in its architecture the church at Ures excelled all the other missions. In Rubí's opinion the garrison at Buenavista could be used to better advantage elsewhere. With the inspection of this presidio, his work in Sonora was finished.

The next phase of Rubí's assignment began on March 16, 1767, when he departed from Buenavista on a journey across the extent of Mexico and Texas to the Louisiana border. Traveling in an easterly and southeasterly direction, Rubí and his party followed a route far to the south of that used in their westward journey. The road or trail over the great Sierra Madre was difficult. Even today, for the most part, it is in the same condition as when Rubí used it. The party passed from the area of Yaqui, Mayo, and Pima missions in Sonora to the land of the Tarahumara missions in Nueva Vizcaya. After twenty-five days of hard riding the travelers reached the Chihuahua road. Retracing the road they had previously used to the valley of San Bartolomé, where there was good pasture, they rested their animals for thirteen days. At this stage of the journey the marqués moved leisurely. From San Bartolomé valley he traveled in one day to Cerro Gordo where he remained twelve days, and then after another one-day journey he reached El Pasaje. Here he remained eight days and finally on May 27, 1767 continued his long trip to Texas.

The initial stages of his route lay south of the Bolsón de Mapimí, a vast unsettled area of mountain and desert, the southern part of which ended in a marshy sink. The region was bounded on the north by the Río Grande and on the east by the Sierra Madre Oriental of Coahuila; on the west it extended almost to the Conchos valley. The only inhabitants of this desolate region were the Apaches, chiefly Mescaleros and Natages, and other wild tribes who came out of this retreat to raid the settlements of Nueva Vizcaya, Coahuila, and even Nueva Galicia to the south. In its northward movement the Spanish frontier had been divided by the Mapimí no man's land. Missionaries and settlers had followed the east corridor on the Coahuila side and the Conchos valley or the Chihuahua-El Paso route on the west.

Four days out of El Pasaje, Rubí reached the pueblo of Alamo, inhabited by about five hundred Tlascaltecas. Formerly they had been established at Parras, but had moved west in 1730 to form the new town. The story of Tlascala and its people is an integral part of the Spanish conquest in Mexico. Without the support of Tlascaltecan allies, Cortés' venture might well have failed. For essential services these Indians were given special privileges and a status in some respects equal to that of Spaniards. In the conquest and occupation of northern Mexico, many of the "Spanish" frontiersmen were Tlascaltecas. Their communities were scattered over Mexico but were most numerous in the northeast. At Alamo they so monopolized the land and water that a number of Spanish inhabitants moved to another site which they named Neuva Bilbao.

The country between Alamo and Saltillo had been occupied by Spaniards for more than a century and a half before Rubí saw it. Despite Apache raids the area was fairly prosperous, and haciendas, ranches, and pueblos were more numerous than in any other region he had visited. Two days' journey brought the party to the pueblo of Santa María de las Parras, which first appeared on the map when

Jesuits from Durango founded a mission there in 1694. Soon thereafter a Tlascaltecan colony arrived and established a pueblo. Rubí discovered that in the past, Tlascaltecan holdings had been encroached upon by two great hacendados who, through political influence and other means, had appropriated much of the best land. One of these was the Marqués de Aguayo who in 1721 had founded Los Adaes, the easternmost presidio of those to be visited by Rubí.

Three days' journey beyond Parras was the dual community of Villa de Santiago del Saltillo and Pueblo de San Estévan de Tlascala. Francisco de Urdiñola established sixty families at Saltillo in the last quarter of the sixteenth century. Later, when the viceroy was sending four hundred Tlascaltecan families to augment settlements on the northern frontier, eighty of them came to Saltillo in 1591, and founded the adjoining pueblo of San Estévan. From this community small groups of settlers in subsequent years were taken into various parts of Coahuila, Nuevo León, and Texas. As Lafora observed, "these Indians speak Spanish and are civilized." In Rubí's time, population of the combined communities amounted to more than eight thousand. The expedition halted for five days at Saltillo, although there was no presidio to inspect.

From Saltillo, Rubí's party turned north to Santiago de la Monclova, passing on the way the boundary line between Nueva Vizcaya and Coahuila. A company of thirty-six cavalrymen was maintained at Monclova, and the captain, Don Jacinto de Barrios y Jáuregui, was governor of the province. Spanish activities in the region were of long duration. Luis de Carabajal had founded Nuevo Almadén near Monclova before the end of the sixteenth century. Almost a century later in 1687 a presidio had been established at Monclova during a period of Indian warfare. Just beyond the town a small Tlascalan pueblo was located adjacent to the mission of San Miguel de Aguayo where there were a few Cohumeros and Timamares Indians.

Upon leaving Monclova, Rubí's next objectives were the presidios of Santa Rosa and San Sabá. Nine days were spent at Santa Rosa and then the party set out for the Río Grande. With the aid of a dugout canoe obtained from a nearby Lipán ranchería, a crossing was made without loss of baggage. However, the strong current caused the loss of a Pausan Indian who was with the company, and two horses. From the Río Grande the party traveled northward to the presidio of San Sabá, passing two small establishments on the road. The first was La Candelaria, which had been constructed by the Franciscans as a mission for the Lipán Apaches, but there were no Apaches in it. The second was the little pueblo of San Lorenzo de la Santa Cruz. Thirty-one soldiers from San Sabá guarded the place, but the two Franciscan missionaries had no Indians in this mission. The inspection party arrived at the presidio of San Luis de las Amarillas, or San Sabá, on July 25, 1767, eight days after crossing the Río Grande. Rubí's instructions stated that "the presidio of San Sabá was established between Texas and New Mexico for the conquest of the Indians who come to attack the provinces of Coahuila and Nueva Vizcaya, and there may be some reason for changing its location." The viceroy directed that "the Señor Marqués, upon his arrival there, shall be careful to advise what he may think." Other documents relative to San Sabá were forwarded to Rubí while he was en route. Consequently the marqués discussed the background and situation of the presidio with Captain Phelipe de Rábago y Terán, its commander.

The history of San Sabá was brief and unhappy. Founded as a mission for the Lipán Apaches, its chief accomplishment had been to incur the animosity of the Comanches and their allies. Franciscan missionaries had hoped that

Comanche pressure on the Apaches would make them more tractable. Military measures had failed to prevent their depredations in the San Antonio region, but there was a bare possibility that missionary efforts might succeed. At any rate a site was selected upon the San Sabá river about 175 miles to the north and west of San Antonio, where soldiers and Franciscans founded presidio San Luis de las Amarillas and Mission San Sabá in 1757. The Apaches displayed little interest, but the Comanches and Taovayas showed too much, for they destroyed the mission before it was a year old. The Franciscans then abandoned the San Sabá location, leaving the presidial garrison with no mission or settled area to guard, a situation unusual and pointless on the frontier. Further missionary efforts at San Lorenzo and Candelaria, to which the Franciscans had gone from San Sabá, failed to convert a single Apache. In the years just prior to Rubí's visit, Comanches had kept the presidio at San Sabá virtually in a state of siege. Rábago urged that the place be abandoned and the field marshal agreed with his opinion and so recommended.[18] After ten days at San Sabá and one Comanche alarm, Rubí departed for San Antonio. Rábago, as a result of Comanche attacks in the following year, moved his garrison south to a less exposed spot at El Cañon. The viceroy reprimanded him for this act but, instead of ordering him to return to San Sabá, sent him and his troops to San Fernando de Austria, a new settlement south of the Río Grande.

Five days' travel from San Sabá brought Rubí and his party to San Antonio de Béjar, largest settlement in Texas. Martín de Alarcón had founded it in 1718 with sixty-two colonists from Coahuila. The growth of the settlement had been stimulated by the recommendations of Pedro de Ri-

18. A detailed report was prepared by Nicolás de Lafora upon the San Sabá situation. It was signed at San Antonio de Béjar, August 12, 1767. A.G.I., Aud. de Guadalajara, 104-6-13 [511].

vera after his great tour of inspection, whereas retrench-
ment resulted in eastern Texas. The presidio of Dolores
was abandoned and Franciscan missionaries of the region
returned to San Antonio where, in 1731, they established
three missions in the adjacent area. In that same year the
Spanish government also transported a colony of Canary
Islanders to San Antonio and founded Villa de San Fernando. In his inspection, Rubí found a presidio, a munici-
pality, and five successful missions established along the
San Antonio valley within a distance of eight miles. Despite its position beyond what the field marshal considered
the best frontier line of defense, and its constant harass-
ment by hostile Indians, the settlement was too firmly established to be moved. Of necessity the presidial garrison
must remain to defend it.

Departing from San Antonio on August 25, 1767, the
Marqués de Rubí began the final segment of his journey to
eastern Texas. Twelve days and many river crossings later
he arrived at the mission of Nacogdoches where he found
one missionary but no neophytes. Lafora commented dryly
that the mission had been in existence for more than forty
years without a single convert. About thirty-five miles beyond Nacogdoches was the mission of Ais which had two
Franciscans but no Indians. Three days' journey beyond
Ais was the presidio of Nuestra Señora del Pilar de los
Adaes, close to the boundary of Louisiana. This outlying
post was the capital of Texas, and the commander of the
cavalry company stationed there was the governor. Fortifications were in poor repair. In the adjoining mission of
San Miguel de Cuéllar de los Adaes there were no Indians. Rubí considered the establishments in eastern Texas
as a needless burden upon the royal treasury.

When France owned Louisiana, a need had existed for
Spain to maintain a foothold in the eastern part of the territory she claimed in Texas. With the cession of Louisiana

to Spain by the treaty of October 9, 1762, danger of French aggression had ceased. Since the time of La Salle, Spanish efforts to occupy Texas had been reflexes to French activities in the Mississippi valley and Gulf region. The founding of Natchitoches on the Red river by St. Denis had caused Spain to establish the presidio of Dolores and missions among the Ais and Adaes Indians a short distance to the west. Eastern Texas was abandoned in 1719 during a war with France. It was reoccupied in 1721 when the Marqués de Aguayo founded the presidio of Los Adaes and placed another garrison at Dolores. Rubí decided that eastern Texas should again be abandoned. Los Adaes was no longer needed to hold an international boundary line and there were no missions to protect because the Indians of the region were not susceptible to propaganda of the faith.

From Los Adaes, Rubí began a five months' return journey to Mexico City. He retraced his route to Nacogdoches and then turned almost directly south, following the trail to presidio San Luis de Ahumada, commonly known as Orcoquizac. After a week spent inspecting the presidio and in making a reconnaissance of the area, he decided that the location was poor because it was too near the Gulf coast where the land was low and swampy. Neither the presidio nor the neighboring mission had any prospect of future development, and this area, in Rubí's opinion, also should be abandoned.

Travel from Orcoquizac to Bahía del Espíritu Santo was slow and difficult. This part of the journey involved crossing the Trinity, San Jacinto, Brazos, Colorado, Guadalupe, and San Antonio rivers, and many smaller streams. The route was much closer to the Gulf than the one followed on the eastern journey, and consequently the crossings were more difficult. That of the Colorado was the worst, requiring two days and resulting in the drowning of seven horses. The party arrived at the presidio of Nuestra Señora de Loreto soon after crossing the San Antonio river near the mission of Espíritu Santo. A road of about fifty miles to the Gulf was impassable in the rainy season. The whole area was low and swampy, and the settlers and soldiers of the presidio suffered greatly from malaria. The missions of the vicinity were not thriving, but at least they had made some converts among the Indians. Ninety-three lived in Espíritu Santo and one hundred and one in the new mission of Nuestra Señora del Rosario, about five miles west of the presidio.

A twelve-day examination of the region caused Rubí to decide that the presidio of Loreto, or Bahía del Espíritu Santo as it was more often called, must be retained despite its unhealthful surroundings. According to Lafora's calculations, it was about seventy leagues due east of San Juan Bautista. Its location, near the coast, was therefore the best available for the last of a chain of presidios extending across the northern border of New Spain from Altar to the Gulf of Mexico. Other reasons for its retention were that Apaches usually did not come that far below San Antonio, and the coastal Indians, generally known as Borrados, were too cowardly to be dangerous and were easily managed by the Franciscans. Rubí commented that they surrendered readily at any show of force and that the missionaries "go to drag them from their hiding places in order to introduce them to the Faith and support their own missions, which could not endure if they were deprived of their recruiting."[19] To protect the road from La Bahía to San Antonio and guard the ranches south of the latter place, Rubí recommended that an officer and twenty men should be stationed at a new post on Arroyo del Cíbolo.

19. Rubí's *dictamen*, April 10, 1768, A.G.I., Aud. de Guadalajara, 104-6-13 [511]).

With his final presidial inspection in Texas completed, Rubí set out on November 12, 1767, for San Juan Bautista del Río Grande in Coahuila. The only settlement along the route was Laredo, a village of sixty huts which straddled the Río Grande. The settlers were armed and organized under a captain of militia, and the community was served by a parish priest. Rubí's party crossed the river at that spot and made the journey into San Juan Bautista in four days. The presidial garrison consisted of thirty-three men, including a captain, lieutenant, and sergeant. Forty families lived adjacent to the presidio, but the settlement was not prosperous because the neighboring missions of San Bernardo and San Juan Bautista had taken over most of the good farm land. Consequently, many people had moved to La Babia and the new town of San Fernando. San Juan Bautista had for many years been the chief gateway to Texas. Louis Juchereau de St. Denis had arrived here in 1714, after an expedition across Texas made in the hope of opening trade between French Louisiana and Mexico. The alarm caused by the appearance of Frenchmen on the Río Grande led to Spain's reoccupation of Texas. Through San Juan Bautista went soldiers, colonists, and pack trains of supplies for the new province. In Rubí's opinion the general location of the presidio was satisfactory, although it would be better for observation purposes if moved a little nearer to the river.

Four days' journey from San Juan brought the inspection party into the New Kingdom of León where settlements and haciendas became more numerous along the route. The expedition arrived at Monterrey, capital of the province, and remained there two weeks. Five hundred families, including those of the military force, comprised the population of the town and the eight haciendas under its jurisdiction. The commander of the garrison was also the governor of the province. Since most hostile tribes of

Indians in Nuevo León had been exterminated and the province was now quite peaceful, the presidio at Monterrey seemed unnecessary.

Rubí departed from Monterrey on December 21, 1767, to finish his last assignment, the inspection of San Francisco Xavier de Valero in the mountainous region of Nayarit. He traveled directly westward to Saltillo. From there, he took the road southwest to Zacatecas rather than the one he had used on his eastward journey which passed through Parras and El Pasaje. The trail to Zacatecas—it was scarcely a road—traversed an arid, rough terrain; a traveler today would find it in about the same condition as it was at that time. Eight days were spent in Mexico's most famous mining town, and then the journey was continued into some of the most rugged parts of the Sierra Madre. En route to Huejuquilla el Alto in the district of Colotlán the party passed several large haciendas in the more fertile valleys. Thirty-two pueblos were in the district. Of these, Huejuquilla el Alto was the largest with a population of 1,500, mostly Indians but a few Spaniards. Beyond the town a short distance was the boundary between Nueva Galicia and Nayarit. The Rubí party next began the gradual ascent to the Mesa del Tonatí. At that place the presidio of San Francisco Xavier stood guard over an Indian population conquered and Christianized for many years, but still not completely trustworthy. Two weeks of inspecting the place caused Rubí to decide that a small detachment should be maintained to police the area, but that a presidio was unnecessary.

When Rubí departed from the Mesa del Tonatí, he had completed his assignment of presidial inspection, but he elected to return to Querétaro by a different route from that he had used previously. Crossing the Camino Real somewhat north of Zacatecas, he took a road to the east of that followed in his northward journey and passed through

La Ciénega Grande and the town of San Miguel el Grande. The former was one of the great Jesuit haciendas where large numbers of horses and mules were bred and production of wheat and corn was considerable. The most significant activity, however, was mining. The hacienda possessed a stamp mill with five ore crushers, several *arrastres,* and all the equipment for extracting silver by the patio process. Ore from adjacent mines yielded about fourteen ounces to the load, which miners considered very good. It was February 12, 1768, when the party passed La Ciénega Grande, and although the King had ordered the expulsion of the Jesuits the preceding year, Lafora made no mention of that fact. From Querétaro, Rubí and his party returned to Mexico City, arriving on February 23, 1768, after a journey of thirty-five months' duration.

Immediately he began work upon his reports. After inspection of each presidio, he had sent to the viceroy and the minister of the Indies, Julián de Arriaga, the information he had collected, together with maps made by Lafora. In the preparation of his reports and recommendations he utilized all pertinent documents at his command.[20] Unfortunately, Rubí had not visited one area he considered especially important in defense of the frontier. That was the valley of the Río Grande below El Paso. His personal observation was limited to his crossing on the way to Texas and his visit to San Juan Bautista on his return. For information upon this region, which he regarded as essential in his defense plans, he relied heavily upon the "reports, charts, and opinions" submitted by Pedro de Rábago y Terán and found by Rubí in the archives of Monclova.[21]

20. Reports and correspondence accumulated during the course of Rubí's inspection amount literally to thousands of pages. Sections 273 and 511 of the Audiencia de Guadalajara, Archivo General de Indias, contain a considerable portion but by no means all of these manuscripts.

21. Rubí's *dictamen,* April 10, 1768, A.G.I., Aud. de Guadalajara, 104-6-13 [511].

Lafora, in his general report of the expedition, also included an excerpt from a diary which Rábago kept while making a reconnaissance from Santa Rosa to La Junta via La Babia and the San Vicente ford of the Río Grande.

Rubí was able to send a report to Arriaga on April 3, and by the 10th had completed the *dictamen* which included his general recommendations. He submitted this document to Viceroy Croix and at the same time forwarded a copy to Arriaga. In the *dictamen*, Rubí reviewed in considerable detail conditions on the frontier and recommended a system of defense which he considered the most effective and also the least burdensome to the royal treasury. A few proposals pertained to routine military matters, such as armament, treatment of soldiers, payment of Indian scouts, and general presidial administration. He meticulously covered all the subjects mentioned in his instructions; beyond that, he earned a place in history by recommending a cordon of fifteen presidios along the northern border of New Spain to defend it against Apaches and other hostile Indians. Commenting upon the significance of Rubí's work, Herbert Eugene Bolton, the great historian of the Spanish Borderlands, wrote as follows:

As a general result of his inspection, which revealed to him some establishments stagnant and useless and others without defense, Rubí concluded—what ought to have been seen long before—that Spain was trying to spread over too much ground, and that a wise policy for her to pursue would be to distinguish between her true and her 'imaginary' domains, and to sacrifice the latter to the former.[22]

In making his recommendations, Rubí had in mind the need for defending New Spain's long frontier with the

22. Herbert Eugene Bolton, *Texas in the Middle Eighteenth Century* (Berkeley, Calif., 1918), p. 379.

small military force available. He explained that he was attempting to establish the shortest line which would protect the northern provinces:

Let us imagine a line (which on the General Map may be shown by dots) drawn from the coast of the Pacific Ocean, beginning between the presidio of El Altar and the ruined mission of San Miguel Sonaytac at about 30 degrees latitude, and extending to the mouth of the Río de Guadalupe on the coast of the Gulf of Mexico, also at 30 degrees north latitude. . . . The difference in longitude between them, according to the most recent maps and observations, is approximately 29 degrees and 15 minutes. Consequently the shortest distance from one point to the other is about 585 leagues. To this imaginary line, which to some extent bounds (disregarding New Mexico for the present) all that may be called the true dominions of the King, we shall try to approximate the real line of defense which it is planned to establish. This, because of the indentations and projections of sierras, lakes and other irregularities of the terrain, may be estimated as approximately 660 leagues in length from end to end.[23]

To create a new defense line upon which presidios should be placed at intervals of about forty leagues, Rubí recommended relocation of twelve presidios. In summary, these changes were as follows: Altar to the mouth of Concepción river, Tubac to the banks of the Santa Cruz, Terrenate to the upper Sobaípuris valley, Fronteras to Santo Domingo valley, San Buenaventura to Laguna Ascensión, El Paso to Carrizal, Guajoquilla to San Eleazario, Julimes to La Junta, Cerro Gordo to San Vicente, San Sabá to Aguaverde, Santa Rosa to the San Rodrigo river, and Monclova to Monclova Viejo. The presidios of Janos, San

23. Rubí's *dictamen*, April, 10, 1768, A.G.I., Aud. de Guadalajara, 104-6-13 [511]. The 585 leagues was considerably underestimated. Rubí's figure of 660 leagues was probably closer to the actual distance.

Juan Bautista, and Bahía del Espíritu Santo had satisfactory locations.

At the time of Rubí's inspection, no presidios were located along the Río Grande from El Paso to San Juan Bautista. The frontier ran below the no man's land of Mapimí. An essential part of his plan was to establish the presidial frontier along the Río Grande north of that unprotected area which permitted raiding Apaches to reach the settlements of Nueva Vizcaya and Nueva Galicia, with little fear of interception or pursuit. The final six new presidial sites which Rubí recommended were on or near the Río Grande below El Paso. His plan pushed New Spain's actual frontier north to that great natural boundary beyond which was Apache land. Some of the new presidial locations were in regions too barren for settlement, but the boundary remained permanently as Rubí drew it.

To finance his plan of frontier defense without putting an additional burden upon the royal treasury, Rubí proposed drastic retrenchments in other areas. He recommended the discontinuance of San Miguel de Horcasitas and Buenavista in Sonora, El Pasaje in Nueva Vizcaya, San Francisco Xavier de Valero in Nayarit, and Monterrey in Nuevo León. For Texas, he recommended the abandonment of the eastern part of the province including the presidios of Los Adaes and San Luis de Ahumada.

Definite estimates of personnel and funds required to implement the plan were submitted in the *dictamen*. Rubí specified that each presidio on the main line of defense should have a garrison of fifty officers and men. Santa Fé and San Antonio were beyond the line but too important to abandon. He therefore recommended that a total of one hundred and sixty officers and men should be assigned to these places and their outposts at Robledo and Arroyo del Cíbolo. Thus a total of nine hundred and sixty soldiers would have the responsibility of guarding New Spain's long frontier. The cost to the royal treasury, according to Rubí's estimate, would be 373,575 pesos per year. Since, at the time of his inspection, the annual budget for presidios was 453,503 pesos, a saving of 79,928 pesos could be accomplished by the adoption of the proposed recommendations.

When Rubí forwarded his *dictamen* to Arriaga from Vera Cruz on May 4, 1768, he commented that the general map which would illustrate his recommendations had not been completed by the two engineers.[24] This map, upon which was shown the "Projecto de su Defensa del Exmo. Don Marqués de Rubí," was approved by the Junta de Guerra and Hacienda which met at Mexico on July 27, 1771. Lafora signed it on August 30, 1771, and it was then forwarded to Spain.[25] A copy, not signed by Lafora, was kept in Mexico. Lafora was Rubí's technical adviser, and without doubt contributed many ideas to the general plan of frontier defenses against the Apaches. After his return to Spain, Lafora was called as an expert witness in 1772 by a junta considering Rubí's recommendations. The council met at the house of the Marqués de Croix, recently the viceroy of New Spain.[26]

In course of the usual deliberate processes of Spanish government, the King issued what is generally known as the "New Regulation of Presidios," dated September 10, 1772, which put into effect practically all of Rubí's recommendations. The first part of this famous document dealt with matters of military organization, supply, equipment, pay, allowances, and duties of officers including those of the inspector-commandant of the Interior Provinces whose

24. Rubí to Arriaga, May 4, 1768, A.G.I., Aud. de Guadalajara, 104-6-13 [511].

25. Alessio Robles, *Nicolás de Lafora*, p. 12, note 2, and map, p. 340.

26. *Ibid.*, p. 18. Also see below, p. 42, note 29.

office was created by the "New Regulation" itself. The second part of the document was titled "Instructions for the New Arrangement of Presidios" and was virtually a summary of Rubí's recommendations. There was one addition. The King ordered the viceroy of New Spain to maintain the old and the new settlements in the Californias. San Diego and Monterey had been founded after Rubí's expedition.[27]

Hugo Oconor, who had served as governor of Texas *ad interim*, was appointed to the position of *inspector-comandante*, and undertook the duty of reorganization of frontier defenses with great energy and courage. He regarded relocation of some of the presidios as unwise; nevertheless, he put the plan into effect wherever possible. Realizing the importance of carrying warfare to the Apaches, he organized campaigns against them in 1773, 1775, and 1776. The first campaign was in the Bolsón de Mapimí and the other two were north of the Río Grande. Oconor's administration was a transition period in which an attempt was made to unify the frontier provinces in a common defense.

Continued warfare upon the frontier caused the Council of the Indies to adopt in 1776 a plan proposed by José de Gálvez, then Minister of the Indies. This separated the Interior Provinces from the viceroyalty of New Spain and placed them under the administration of a *comandante general*. Teodoro de Croix who was appointed to the office made another inspection of the frontier in the years 1777-1778 and discovered that conditions differed little from those of the previous decade. Creation of the Provincias

27. *Reglamento é instrucción para los presidios que se han de formar en la linea de frontera de la Nueva España. Resuelto por el Rey N. S. en cédula de 10 de Septiembre de 1772.* First printed in Madrid, 1772. Reproduced in Arrillaga, *Recopilación de Leyes* . . . (Mexico, 1835), IX, 139-189.

Internas for a time unified defense efforts but resulted in no marked advance beyond Rubí's line of presidios.[28]

Rubí's inspection and his recommendations were significant in that they focused attention upon the condition of the Interior Provinces and indicated where a stand should be taken against Apache incursions. Despite all subsequent Spanish military efforts, the actual northern boundary of New Spain remained permanently where Rubí and Lafora had drawn it and the New Regulation of 1772 had confirmed it.[29]

28. New Spain's northern frontier defense history after 1772 is found in many publications, of which the following present basic source material and are outstanding. A. B. Thomas, *Teodoro de Croix and the Northern Frontier of New Spain, 1776-1783,* and Donald E. Worcester, *Instructions for Governing the Interior Provinces of New Spain, 1786* (The Quivira Society, Berkeley, Calif., 1951).

29. Several contemporary copies of Lafora's map of the northern frontier of New Spain were made. For a partial list see Carl Irving Wheat, *Mapping the Transmississippi West, 1540-1861* (San Francisco, 1957), Vol. I, pp. 88, 89. Herbert E. Bolton in *Texas in the Middle Eighteenth Century* (p. 382) published the eastern portion of a signed copy deposited in the Archivo General de Indias, Sevilla. He refers (p. 378) to another copy which has disappeared from Volume V, Sección de Historia, Archivo General y Público, Mexico. Many Lafora and Urrutia maps are published in a great series of volumes, *Cartografía de Ultramar* (1949—), by the Servicio Geográfico e Histórico del Ejército, Madrid, Spain. A copy of Lafora's frontier map is in the Cartographic Records Branch of the National Archives, Washington, D. C. Formerly it was in the possession of the War Department and may have been brought from Mexico by the United States Army after the Treaty of Guadalupe Hidalgo. It was an intriguing coincidence that the international boundary line of 1848 followed with so few variations the line of New Spain's northern defenses established in 1772. William H. Emory in his *Report* on the United States and Mexican Boundary Survey stated that "under Spanish dominion, a cordon of military and ecclesiastical stations extended from sea to sea" and emphasized its significance. *House of Representatives, 34th Congress, 1st Session, Executive Document No. 135* (Washington, D. C., 1857), Vol. I, Part I, pp. 68-69.

REPORT

OF THE JOURNEY

WHICH, BY ORDER OF THE MOST EXCELLENT VICEROY,

THE MARQUÉZ DE CRUILLAS,

WAS MADE BY

THE CAPTAIN OF ENGINEERS, DON NICOLÁS DE LA FORA,

IN COMPANY WITH THE FIELD MARSHAL,

THE MARQUÉZ DE RUBÍ,

UNDER COMMISSION FROM HIS MAJESTY

TO REVIEW THE INTERIOR PRESIDIOS

SITUATED ON THE FRONTIER OF THE PART OF NORTH

AMERICA BELONGING TO THE KING.

INTRODUCTION TO THE WORK AND
REASONS FOR THE JOURNEY

The part of North America in whose discovery and conquest the Spanish name became immortal is the subject of the following diary. I have endeavored to formulate it with the greatest care to detail, observing minutely in my long and arduous journey whatever may contribute to giving a distinct and clear idea of His Majesty's dominions. I have not refrained from making the most profound reflections upon the character of the enemies who infest the frontiers, and upon their manner of making war, and that of the presidial soldiers, in order to deduce the reason why the former are so audacious and the latter of so little use. I shall explain the reason for this state of affairs in a dissertation with which I propose to close the work. I shall prescribe, as far as my limited understanding permits, an easy and certain method of preventing the tremendous damage which His Majesty's subjects suffer daily from the barbarians, and of bringing the latter under subjection by making our arms respected in those remote countries. The King, having been informed of the constant complaints of those unhappy frontier subjects through the representations of their superior government and being anxious to find a remedy, sent the Field Marshal Marqués de Rubí to inspect all the interior presidios. The Marqués de Cruillas thought that it might be an advantage for the Field Marshal to be accompanied by an engineer who would devote himself to making a descriptive map of those immense territories which up to now have been badly surveyed and even more poorly described. He selected me for this commission, and I have given the greatest care and personal labor in order to carry out the project.

MARCH, 1766

To Tepozotlán.

On the 18th of March I left Mexico. Having traveled north and north northwest the distance of seven leagues, I stopped for the night in Tepozotlán. The population is composed of Spaniards, Indians, mestizos, and mulattoes. There is a school, which was a novitiate of the Jesuit fathers, whose architecture has neither taste nor design. The road is level and good, with the exception of one slope which is full of loose gravel.

To Tepexe del Río.

On the 19th I went to Tepexe del Río, traveling principally to the east, over a distance of six leagues through a hilly country which was almost impassable for carriages on account of its innumerable rocks. Indians compose the greater number of its inhabitants, and the rest are Spaniards, mestizos, and mulattoes. This pueblo, small in size, is situated in a fairly pleasant little valley with a small stream running through it.

To the Pueblo of San Francisco.

On the 20th I traveled six leagues and stopped at the small pueblo of San Francisco, inhabited by Otomí Indians, as is that of Clauda which I reached two leagues beyond Tepexe. This road is tolerable, but a short distance north of the former town the footing becomes very uncomfortable due to loose rock, which is increasingly bad on the Clauda hill. The hill covers a league in which there are several very sharp slopes, and is scarcely passable on wheels. The ascent is to the northwest. From the top the road continues west and is somewhat more passable although it is still very bad because of the great amount of stone and rock. This stretch of country is commonly called "bad lands."

To Ruano.

On the 21st I traveled six leagues to Ruano. At the end of the first two, traveling northwest, one comes to the small town of Capulalpa. Immediately beyond it is a grade of the same name, full of stones and rocky declivities, but quite short. Two leagues farther on is the hacienda of Arroyo Zarco, where there were plenty of horses and small livestock when it belonged to the Jesuits. One travels this distance to the northwest, one quarter to the west, and the same for the remaining two leagues to Ruano. Half way there is the small rancho Las Encinillas, where a small crop of maize is raised on a small portion of land alloted to this purpose. The rest of the land in the vicinity is used for pasturage only. The rancho Ruano consists of a dozen huts thatched with a long grass which they call *zacate*. To the left of it there is a pond of water which, with other springs, forms the San Juan river. Leaving Arroyo Zarco one comes upon a river bed which contains water only in rainy season. Climbing the small rise on the other side one sees at a short distance to the right of the road, a small lagoon formed by a spring where drinking water is obtained throughout most of the year.

To San Juan del Río and thence to Querétaro.

On the 22nd I traveled six leagues to the northwest, with slight inclination toward the west during the first five, over the Cazadero plain, so called because of a celebrated hunt of wild beasts of all species put on by the natives in honor of one of the most Excellent Viceroys, who was shown thousands of animals gathered together in this plain which is five leagues wide. There are two roads; one by way of the Venta del Cuervo, and the other, which I followed, by way of Las Palmillas. There the two roads meet near a deserted and ruined house which bears the latter

MILITARY PLAZA, SAN ANTONIO, TEXAS

THE PLAZA AND CHURCH OF EL PASO

FALLS OF PRESIDIO DE RÍO GRANDE

Quivira Society

LIPÁN CROSSING, 85 MILES ABOVE THE MOUTH OF THE PECOS

A LIPÁN WARRIOR

VIEW OF PRESIDIO DE SAN VICENTE AND SIERRA CARMEL

MISSION CONCEPCIÓN, TEXAS

PRESIDIO OF SAN ELEAZARIO

SCENE AT THE TOWN OF FRONTERAS

GROUP OF APACHE WARRIORS

VIEW OF MAGDALENA, SONORA

A CARAVAN APPROACHING THE PRESIDIO OF JANOS

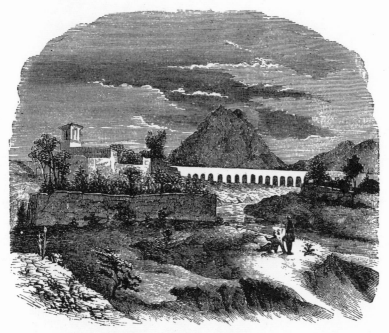

AQUEDUCT AND CHURCH OF SANTA RITA, CHIHUAHUA CITY

PUEBLO OF SAN FELIPE, NEW MEXICO

MIMBRES RIVER VALLEY, NEW MEXICO

THE CITY OF SANTA FÉ, NEW MEXICO

name. A small slope follows. It is covered with loose rock as is the last league to San Juan del Río.

This place, inhabited by Spaniards, Indians, mestizos, and mulattoes, has in all probability about four hundred houses, all low and level with the street, the greater part of them adobe. In it are a parochial church served by a cleric, a Dominican monastery, and a convent of the same order. There are some stores which sell merchandise and there is a good deal of traffic, because one has to pass through this place in order to reach the interior. For this reason the greater part of its inhabitants devote themselves to blacksmithing. The town is situated on the right bank of an unnamed river, which carries a very small amount of water, and can be forded in the dry season. For rainy season, when it is full of water, a well constructed bridge with five arches has been built.

Everywhere along the road there are droves of horses and some small ranches.

Five leagues from Ruano is the pueblo of Guichiapa, and ten from San Juan del Río is that of Tolimanejo. Because they are both in the Sierra Gorda adjacent to the rebellious Mecos Indians, a squadron of soldiers from the colony of Nuevo Santander is maintained at the last named pueblo.

On the 23rd I traveled ten leagues on a course midway between west and northwest, over good level road except on leaving San Juan, where there is a small slope and a rocky stretch of road. After La Noria, which is two leagues this side of Querétaro, the road continues to be hilly and rocky as far as the city.

A league and a half from San Juan, on the right, is the Estancia Grande site. Here there is a great deal of farm land with horses, and some sheep. At five leagues is La Lira. Thence to Querétaro it is five more leagues. In this vicinity there is much nopal and some mesquite, and an occasional well furnishes the only water.

Querétaro.

The city of Querétaro is situated on the bank of a river containing very little water in the dry season. The country surrounding it is a plain with sierras on all sides. Here the heat is extremely severe. Very good fruit is produced, and there is much farm land well-suited for all kinds of grain. There are several houses on the plain. The population of Querétaro exceeds 14,000 souls, governed in temporal matters by a mayor and in spiritual by a parish priest, both subject to the respective jurisdictions of Mexico. Of this number, 1,000 of the Spaniards and mestizos were enlisted for the five militia cavalry companies of fifty-four men each, exclusive of Indians and mulattoes, which were assembled by the Marqués de Rubí under superior order.

Most of the houses are adobe. Among them are ten convents for friars, three for nuns, and several churches, which, on account of their superior height, show prominently above the low roofs of the other houses. There is abundant water carried across a very wide valley by an aqueduct on arches.

For certain reasons I remained there the 24th and 25th. Taking advantage of this time, I made observations of the sun and found this city to be situated in 20°47′ north latitude, and I assigned to it 269° longitude, counting from the Tenerife meridian, according to printed tables. I do not know how accurate this is. Since I had neither instruments nor time to perform this calculation, I could not verify it.

To Celaya.

On the 26th I traveled ten leagues over level land, uncultivatable because of mesquite and briars. The first six leagues to the west led to the Indian pueblo of San Juan Bautista de Apaseo. In that distance there is only one small slope covered with loose rock, about a league from Querétaro. The remaining four leagues to the city of Celaya are over level ground, west, one quarter northwest. In the whole distance the only water, except that found in some wells, is a spring near Apaseo. This is a small Indian pueblo in which all the houses are adobe and low. So are those of Celaya, with the exception of some on the plaza, which have an upper story. Its size approximates that of Querétaro, but its surroundings are more agreeable because of the many olive trees. They produce very good olives. There is little water, but they supplement this lack with a great number of wells, from which water as necessary is drawn by means of *bimbaletes*.

Celaya has five companies of militia cavalry, each composed of fifty-four men. There is an alcalde mayor, and a parish priest ministers to them. There is also a monastery of considerable size belonging to the Franciscan Fathers.

To Salamanca.

On the 27th I traveled nine leagues, the first four west over good level road, the whole surrounding country being green and well cultivated as far as El Guaje inn, where the little Laja river passes. This river always has some water and flows toward Salamanca where it empties into the Río Grande. The next five leagues I traveled to the west one quarter to the northwest over level land, although less cultivated than the first-named on account of its poorer quality. In the wet season, especially along the sides of the road, there is nothing but brush and swamp.

There are many people in Salamanca but few of them are white. There are probably a thousand houses, all adobe and low. Standing above them are the parochial church, served by a parish priest, and an Augustinian monastery.

The town is situated on the bank of the Río Grande [Lerma], which rises near Lerma. It flows by Salamanca, Guadalajara, and Colima, and empties into the South Sea at San Blas. The people of this settlement of Salamanca are subject to an alcalde mayor.

To Silao.

On the 28th I traveled twelve leagues, four of them over level ground to the north as far as the small pueblo of Temascatío. The Puerto Blanco, a small range, begins there, and the road runs in the same direction over some rocky stretches to the top. This distance is a league and a half, and half-way is the Sierra rancho. Here there is an arroyo where a number of pools collect which supply water in dry season. From the summit the road turns west and divides into two, the right branch leading to Real de Minas de Guanajuato, and the other continuing for a quarter of a league to the rancho called Troje Blanca. From there it runs northwest for another quarter of a league as far as Las Caleras. It is crossed by a little stream with several pools, which supply the people of Troje Blanca with water. From Las Caleras to Silao it is six leagues over level ground with the exception of a small slope at the beginning. The whole country is well cultivated and produces an abundance of maize, beans, chile, and some wheat. At the same time there is no lack of pasture to feed the many herds of horses and cattle. Silao is a place of considerable size. There is a community of 8,000 souls, counting Indians and whites. The houses are of adobe and low. There is a good-sized parochial church with its chapel, and several other churches and chapels, administered by a parish priest.

To the Town of León.

On the 29th I traveled seven leagues northwest over level ground and an occasional low hill. At the end of three leagues is Los Sauces rancho. Four leagues from it is the town of León. There is much pasture in the vicinity of this road and plenty of farm land.

The settlement of León consists of about 3,000 houses. It has ten churches, including those of the Jesuits and Franciscans who control this curacy. The arrangement of the houses is the same as in the pueblos before named, with the difference that many are built of stone. There is no water except from wells.

To Lagos.

On the 30th I traveled eight leagues, principally northwest. At the start there is a three-league climb over many very sharp slopes covered with loose rock up to Las Lagunillas. The district of Nueva Galicia begins at this place. At Las Lagunillas the road divides, and the one to the left is a carriage road. Half a league along, just before a very troublesome rocky slope, there are some Indian huts called El Saucillo. Along the remaining four and a half leagues to Lagos there are a number of hills, whose ravines and cliffs are extremely difficult to cross. It is also very difficult to cross the sandy stretch between the two branches of the river near the town.

All of this territory, because it is mountainous, is useful only to raise mules and horses, and there are a number of farms in the vicinity for this purpose.

The town of Lagos is composed of some three or four hundred low adobe houses, forming several parallel streets. There is a parochial church, a monastery of the Order of La Merced, and another of the Capuchins. A great number of Indian huts or cabins are scattered throughout the neighborhood. The inhabitants are Indians, mulattoes, mestizos, and some Spaniards. They are administered by the parish priest and governed by an alcalde mayor, subject to the audiencia of Guadalajara.

The river [San Juan de los Lagos] according to the custom of the country, varies its name, taking the names of the places through which it passes. It rises in some mountains six leagues above Comange [de Corona] and flows by the Ibarra hacienda. When it reaches Lagos it is augmented by the water from a canal proceeding from a medium-sized lake which is half a league from the town. The canal was constructed for the use of a mill. The river continues its course by way of Guadalajara to the South Sea. Usually it contains only a very small amount of water, but it is an obstruction to travelers in the wet season when it cannot be forded.

On the 31st I did not travel. Having taken observations, I found the location of this town to be in 21°39' latitude, and 267°20' longitude.

APRIL

To the Hacienda of Los Sauces.

On the 1st I traveled eight leagues following a general course north-northwest through mountainous country. After half a league I came to the lake of which I have spoken. In its vicinity maize, beans, and wheat are sown and produce in great abundance. One league from Lagos is the village of Buena Vista. After passing this, one comes to a slope called El Portezuelo, at the foot of which is the hacienda of Doña María Guerra. After a number of hills and descents, at the beginning of the last climb is the Mariquita river bed formed from several springs during rainy season. One finally reaches the hacienda Los Sauces on the bank of an arroyo which is never dry and has its source in springs in the Ciénaga de Matas, six leagues away.

To the Town of Aguas Calientes.

On the 2nd I traveled nine leagues in a direction halfway between north and northwest over ground similar to the above. At the end of four leagues is the hacienda San Bartolomé. Here wheat, maize, and chile are harvested in proportion to the water which is stored by a dam for irrigation. They also have a well and a creek which retains some pools in dry season to provide for the small number of livestock. The remaining five leagues as far as Aguas Calientes pass through the same sort of country. This land is useful only as pasture.

The town of Aguas Calientes, composed of 2,000 houses, not counting the Indian huts surrounding it, is situated in a well-cultivated plain, with much farm land. Chile, maize, and beans are produced in abundance as well as wheat. One league to the east there is a medicinal hot spring. It forms an arroyo which passes by the town and is used in irrigating a number of orchards and chile pepper fields. Another league to the west, at the place called Morcinique, there is another spring from which drinking water is obtained by means of two buckets on a pulley. This town has an agreeable appearance for the houses are in a grove of trees. As the houses are low, like those of the towns previously mentioned, and made of the same material, a better effect is produced by the six churches among them. Three of these belong to the orders of La Merced, San Juan de Dios, and San Diego, and the others are administered by clerics. To this class belongs the parish priest who ministers to mulattoes, Indians, mestizos, and Spaniards. There are also a number of stores managed by Europeans which sell merchandise. All are governed by an alcalde mayor.

The bed of the river, which has water only when it rains, is at the entrance to the town.

To the Hacienda of El Pabellón.

On the 3rd I traveled eight leagues to the north over level ground, with an occasional small rise. Twice I crossed

dry-shod over the San Pedro river, which passes by Aguas
Calientes and joins the Santiago river. There was scarcely
any water in it. On reaching the first rancho the road divides. I took the one to the left leading to the hacienda El
Pabellón, where the road turns toward Zacatecas.

One league from Aguas Calientes is the hacienda called
Pozo Bravo; another league beyond is the Indian rancho
called Chicalote. A short distance from the road there are
several other haciendas surrounded by farm lands. The
rest is nothing but pasture and cactus where many mules
and horses are raised. These animals, together with some
farm land, are the property of the hacienda El Pabellón.

To the Hacienda of San Pedro.

On the 4th I traveled eight leagues in a general course
north-northeast over level ground with plenty of pasturage
and cacti. The rancho Saucillo is at the end of the first two
leagues.

It is two more leagues from this rancho to that of La
Punta, and a short distance from there the road branches.
The one running north goes to Tlacotes; the other, which
I followed, goes west to the hacienda San Pedro. The latter consists of farm lands, irrigated by damming a stream
originating three leagues away in mountains which extend
to Zacatecas. At San Pedro there are a great many mules
and some sheep.

To Zacatecas.

On the 5th I traveled ten leagues, the first four over a
plain of the same nature as the preceding, bearing to the
northeast as far as Las Palmillas. The other six leagues to
Zacatecas, traveling west-northwest, I followed a general
course over hilly country whose steepness and roughness
increase right up to the city itself.

The city is situated on four slopes at the confluence of two gorges. It has a parochial church and five monasteries of the orders of San Francisco, Santo Domingo, San Agustín, and San Juan de Dios. There was also a very rich Jesuit college. Because of the decline of the mines, formerly heavy producers, there are very few friars. For the same reason the population has diminished considerably, totalling only 6,778 communicants and 4,300 children, including Spaniards, Indians, mestizos, and mulattoes. In neighboring haciendas there are probably 500 persons.

The 6th and 7th I remained at Zacatecas. After taking observations twice I found it to be in north latitude 22° 59,' and 265° 50' longitude, by the Tenerife meridian. It is surrounded by several mountain ranges, some more distant than others. Among them a flat-topped rock called La Bufa stands out.

To Fresnillo.

On the 8th I traveled twelve leagues on a general route northwest. The ground was level with an abundance of pasturage and nopal except at the exit of the town where it is hilly for the space of a league. At the end of five leagues is La Calera. The road continues over a plain up to within two leagues of Fresnillo where there are also hills and loose rocks which the people call El Portezuelo de la Estanzuela. Before that, one comes to Las Tapias three leagues from La Calera. At the foot of the latter there is a little stream where there are a few pools in dry season. From here it is four leagues to Fresnillo, one of the most important mining towns. The population here, counting all classes, totals 3,000 persons and is administered by a parish priest whose tithes amount to 12,000 pesos. There are four churches.

To La Escondida.

On the 9th I traveled ten leagues on a general route north-northwest over level ground with abundant pasture where horses and sheep are raised. At the end of six leagues is the Río del Tolosa or Medina, which contains half a *vara* of water. On its banks are about a dozen huts occupied by mestizos. Four leagues beyond is the small rancho La Escondida.

To the Hacienda of Calahorra.

On the 10th I traveled ten leagues on a general course northwest over hilly country abounding in pasture and nopal and some rough stretches. At the end of five leagues is the hacienda Atotonilco situated in a little valley where there is some farm land. A quarter of a league beyond is another hacienda and a small Indian pueblo, all on the banks of a small arroyo. Five leagues farther on is the hacienda Calahorra which also has farm lands.

To the Town of Llerena or Mining Town of Sombrerete.

On the 11th I traveled ten leagues over rocky hills. At the end of four leagues I came to Villa de Llerena or the mining town of Sombrerete, half-ruined by the decline of the mines. La Noria, the only one left, produces some silver. The mining town is situated in the midst of several mountain ranges at a considerable elevation. Houses are low and about five hundred in number, although many of them are in ruins. There are two monasteries, one Franciscan and the other Dominican, and a parochial church with several chapels attended by a parish curate and several priests. The water, abundant and of good quality, comes through a flume of hollowed logs.

Over our road one travels west and west-northwest for six leagues before reaching the hacienda El Calabazar. On leaving the mining town one comes to a very steep rocky hill a quarter of a league long. Then the road, which is quite long, is almost level to the descent to the aforesaid hacienda. The hacienda is situated in a valley formed by very high and rugged mountains. There may be as many as two hundred persons there employed in cultivating a little maize and caring for some horses, cattle, and a few sheep. Everywhere in this vicinity there is abundant pasture and thick woods.

To the Hacienda of Juana Guerra.

On the 12th I traveled nine leagues principally to the west-northwest. At the end of the first three leagues over a very good road, except for a stretch at the start, I came to the Muleros hacienda. There are plenty of pasturage and woods in this vicinity and as far as the hacienda Juana Guerra six leagues farther on. Two leagues from Muleros is the Graseros river, containing so little water that at times it does not flow. This river flows toward the town of Nombre de Dios which is one league west of the hacienda Juana Guerra.

The Town of El Nombre de Dios.

At the town of Nombre de Dios as well as at the hacienda Muleros the soil is irrigated with spring water and some maize is sown. At the first hacienda many mulattoes are employed in the care of the large number of horses there. In the second there are no more than forty persons. The number of inhabitants in the town is reduced to a few Spaniards, a few more mulattoes, and eight hundred Mexican Indians. This pueblo is divided by a canal. The people are administered by a parish priest and are governed by an alcalde mayor. All this road is almost level, passing through the valley which begins at the hacienda El Calabazar.

To the Small Rancho Los Berros.

On the 13th I traveled nine leagues, principally northwest, through country like that of the previous day, until I reached the small rancho Los Berros, situated on the banks of a small stream. Following the same woods for a league and a half from La Punta, I covered the remaining six leagues to the hacienda La Punta, which belonged to the Jesuits. Along this last stretch there are some bad lands that are almost impassable. It is necessary to take a guide who knows how to skirt around them. The hacienda is located on the banks of a river also called La Punta. Its chief industry is horse raising.

To Durango.

On the 14th I traveled eight leagues in a northwesterly direction over well-wooded level land with abundant pasture. On leaving La Punta one fords the river of this name and after skirting around a small hill with some stretches of bad lands one comes out upon the highway which is a fine road. The Santiago river, which has very little water, is crossed at the end of two leagues. It unites with La Punta river. At a short distance is La Sauceda river, which was dry, and finally, three leagues from Durango, one comes to El Tunal river. On its banks along the same road is the hacienda San Miguel. At this hacienda there are a great many horses, cattle, and some sheep. They graze on a plain which, with a little trouble, could be irrigated by the water from El Tunal.

The city of Durango, also called Guadiana, is the capital of Nueva Vizcaya, and is the present residence of the governor. It has a cathedral with its bishop and canons and three monasteries of the friars of San Francisco, San Agustín, and San Juan de Dios. There was a Jesuit college and also some more small churches. There is also a royal treasury where the "fifth" on the silver from Sonora and Chihuahua is paid. The population is made up of 1,311 families, including Spaniards, mulattoes, and mestizos, with 8,937 communicants. In the village of Analco, which is close by and may be considered as a suburb, there are ninety-five Indian families totaling 610 persons. Durango is situated in a beautiful plain, entirely uncultivated because of lack of water, which could be easily brought from El Tunal, as I have already said. An attempt was made to bring it into the city by aqueduct, but the plan was dropped soon afterwards on account of the cost. The section that had been constructed was left abandoned as useless. Near the city is a very abundant spring, but it is not fit for drinking and has been diverted to irrigating some orchards. Water is conducted through several ditches which pass through the streets. The overflow forms a swamp outside the city, allowing the water to be wasted when it could be used. The greater part of the houses are low, on a level with the street where they are arranged parallel, and their appearance is in no way attractive. Very good grapes and excellent peaches are produced. There are great extremes of temperature according to the seasons. In summer this country is made uninhabitable by the prodigious number of scorpions, so poisonous that their sting kills even adults. Children escape only by luck. Nor is there any lack of tarantulas and centipedes whose poison is also deadly.

In this city I overtook the Marqués de Rubí who was waiting for me. As some time was necessary to replenish our supplies and rest the mules, we remained there until the 26th. During all this time I was able to take only one observation of the sun, for it was constantly cloudy at noon and even on that one occasion it was somewhat overcast and I could not verify the observation. I found its north latitude to be 24°9,' and the longitude commonly assigned to it 264,° west of the Tenerife meridian.

To Avino.

On the 26th we traveled eighteen leagues over level land covered with mesquites, huizaches, and pasturage. Ten leagues' travel to the northeast is the hacienda El Chorro. On leaving this place one comes to a small swamp. Traveling eight leagues north one arrives at Avino. One league before reaching Avino there is a slope near the hacienda Santo Domingo de la Boca. The latter is situated at the entrance of a gap between two mountain ranges. The road leading to Avino passes through this gap. The town is in a hollow among some hills. It is a mining camp which yields a fair amount of silver. For this reason as many as two thousand persons have congregated in it including Spaniards, mestizos, and mulattoes.

On the 27th we did not travel and after making observations I found this hacienda to be situated in 24°46′ north latitude, and in 264°30′ longitude.

To the Hacienda of Santa Catarina.

On the 28th we went to the hacienda of Santa Catarina, seven leagues distant to the northeast on a general course. The first two leagues are over a very bad road, hilly and full of gorges and rocks up to the small swamp of Santa Gertrudis, or Avino. At this point the horse trail branches off crossing some hills shortening the distance, for it is only three leagues to Santa Catarina, and by the coach road it is five. The principal reason for establishing this hacienda is sheep shearing. As many as 130,000 head of sheep are driven in for annual shearing. There are 7,000 mares for breeding horses and mules. There are 2,000 inhabitants, for whose sustenance twenty-five bushels of corn are planted as well as some beans. There are two small springs of drinking water and two ponds for sheep and cattle, for there are also some of the latter.

To the Hacienda of El Alamo.

On the 29th we traveled nine leagues on a direct course
north over low hills with a great deal of pasturage, and
here and there mesquite on the slopes. At three leagues
we came to the rancho Las Tortuguillas, and after six more
to the hacienda El Alamo. The latter is simply a summer
pasture for cattle. Nothing else is produced. There are
ninety families, including servants. El Alamo is situated on
the banks of a small stream of the same name which has
very little water. It rises in Las Tortuguillas in a place
called Las Tapias and empties into the Nasas river.

To the Presidio of El Pasaje.

On the 30th we went to the presidio of La Limpia Concepción del Pasaje. We traveled ten leagues over hills
thickly covered with low mesquite, huizaches, cat's claws,
tasajos, etc., but very little grass. At the start the road runs
northeast, and then turns north-northwest, entering a valley formed by several extremely rugged mountain ranges.
Four leagues before the presidio is the small Chupaderos
rancho. There is another way by horse which cuts over the
hills and reduces the distance to not more than seven
leagues. This trail passes through Cañón de Culantrillo
and rancho Las Burras.

The plan I made of this presidio will show its shape,
arrangement, and the materials of its construction. In the
vicinity, which was impossible to include in the plan, there
are very high mountain ranges in every direction except to
the northeast. In that direction the road leads to Cuencamé
over gentle slopes, which together form an approximate
circle, ending in the plain where the presidio is situated.
The company which garrisons it is composed of a captain,
a lieutenant, a sergeant, and thirty-three soldiers who are
employed in escorting an occasional traveler, in carrying

official communications, and other even less important tasks. For this reason I think the presidio might be abandoned. Otherwise it will probably end in ruining the Count of San Pedro del Alamo, at whose expense it exists by contract with his Majesty, without conducing in any way to the public good or safe-guarding the country, since it is situated far to the rear, as may be seen in the general map.

MAY

It was necessary for us to remain here to review this presidio until the 14th of this month, when we set out. We traveled fourteen leagues almost northwest, over level ground covered with low trees, mesquites, huizaches, cat's claws, etc., and here and there a stretch of loose rocks. Four leagues farther is the arroyo or watering place of La Vieja, which is the only one in all this journey. Four leagues more led us to the small pass of La Tinaja, which was six leagues from the hacienda San Antonio, where we stopped. This hacienda is situated on the bank of the Nasas river, which is formidable in flood time. It empties into the Laguna de Parras. The road followed on this day goes through a valley formed by two chains of very high mountains. In its widest part the valley is about one league wide. The mountain range on the right is called El Rosario.

To the Pueblo El Gallo, formerly a Presidio.

On the 15th we traveled twelve leagues to the northwest, one quarter west, taking a general route over ground like the preceding. At a quarter of a league is the place called La Plazuela de los Arrieros, where we crossed the almost dry river. It is divided into several branches. Then one enters an almost circular plain surrounded by several high, bare mountain ranges, precipitous in many places and of very extraordinary shapes. These mountains allow passage to a narrow valley called La Baquilla. This is six leagues from San Antonio and another six from the abandoned presidio El Gallo. This ground is another plain similar to the first. It extends to a small hill, from whose summit the town may be seen. This place has a population of eight hundred persons who live in low adobe houses. Its former appearance may still be perceived from various fragments forming a square plaza, with two circular towers diagonally opposite to defend the side walls. Three of these walls were formed by the houses themselves, and on the fourth side, where the principal entrance was, there were some rooms which served as a guard house. According to Brigadier Don Pedro de Ribera it is situated in 26°3′ north latitude. The Nasas river rises in the Sierra Madre, in the neighborhood of El Zape mission and hacienda Cestin, 45 leagues from El Gallo, and its course runs from southwest northeast until it disappears in Laguna de Parras.

To La Zarca de Arriba.

On the sixteenth we traveled sixteen leagues northwest one quarter west on a general course over level, arid land, where we saw some wild palms but very little grass. Not a single watering place was found until we came to Carrizal creek, two leagues before reaching the hacienda La Zarca de Arriba. There we halted. At this place and at La Zarca de Abajo, about a quarter of a league away, there are 250 persons. They are employed in raising horses, mules, cattle, and sheep, the occupation of these haciendas.

To Cerro Gordo, Abandoned Presidio.

On the 17th we went to the abandoned presidio of Cerro Gordo. We traveled ten leagues northwest over ground similar to the above. The few remaining fragments of the old ruins did not show the plan, which doubtless must have been like that of El Gallo. Its location is on the edge of a very deep gorge, through which passes a stream formed by two creeks. Half a league farther up these unite. One rises in the Tramojos sierra, six leagues to the southwest. The other rises in Mimbrera, four leagues to the west, and flows on to disappear in the marshes at the foot of Sierra Pozo Hediondo twenty leagues to the north. There is an alcalde mayor, whose jurisdiction includes the San Juan Bautista hacienda, the Estancia del Carrizo, the pueblos La Mimbrera, and El Tascate, whose populations will come to about a hundred persons, most of them mulattoes.

On the 18th we did not travel.

To the Rancho of La Asunción.

On the 19th we traveled fourteen leagues northwest over ground like the preceding. At five leagues is La Parida waterhole, and five leagues farther on Alamo creek. Four leagues from the latter is the cattle ranch Nuestra Señora de la Asunción on the bank of the Florido river, which flows from southwest to northeast. On its verdant banks there are several haciendas.

To the Valley of San Bartolomé.

On the 20th we traveled ten leagues to the northwest over ground like the preceding. In a distance of six leagues we crossed dry-shod over the arroyos of San Agustín, Los Mimbres, and Balsequillo, all with very little water. It is five leagues to the lower end of the hacienda La Concepción. From this place to San Bartolomé valley is five more leagues. Two leagues before reaching it one crosses the Enmedio river. All day long we had on our right, for six leagues, a mountain chain between that of Baos range and the Peñoles range. From these mountains enemy Indians are in the habit of attacking the haciendas which lie be-

tween the valley and the Florido river. This could easily
be prevented by the Guajoquilla presidio. The location of
this area and the places from whence the Indians attack
show distinctly on the map I made of this section of the
country.

The place called Valle de San Bartolomé is situated in
27°19′ north latitude and in 261°30′ longitude by the
Tenerife meridian. In it are a parish priest and an alcalde
mayor. Their jurisdiction is probably seventy leagues in
circumference including Las Bocas, a pueblo exclusively of
Tarahumares Indians which is located approximately
south of the Florido river. The boundary comes from this
pueblo, runs east of Cabecera and goes on by way of Guajoquilla to unite with the Conchos. Then it separates from
the Conchos and, after cutting across the Parral river, re-
turns to close up the circle at the same Las Bocas. Previous
to this, one comes to the Santa Barbara river, later called
Enmedio. After it crosses part of the jurisdiction it empties
into the Florido.

On the banks of the Florido there are four haciendas;
four more along the Balsequillo, which crosses the district
from west to east; six are on the banks of the Santa Barbara or Enmedio, which runs in the same direction as the
preceding; seven on the Parral, which flows in the same
direction and whose waters are entirely used in irrigation
of these haciendas. Midway between the last-named and
the Conchos river is an arroyo which comes down from the
sierra of Las Animas, following the same course as the
others. Its water is used to irrigate five haciendas. In the
center of the district, two leagues from the settlement of
San Bartolomé, there is a spring which forms a stream
that flows through the town. Although some of the water
is taken out to irrigate a good many orchards, there is still
enough for the fourteen haciendas situated on its banks
along the whole length of the valley through which it flows.

Its course terminates at the last hacienda. In the capital and haciendas above mentioned there are 4,751 persons, counting Spaniards, mestizos, and mulattoes who enjoy this verdant country. There are in abundance various fruits of Spain, among them very good grapes. They harvest much maize, beans, wheat, some barley, and a little wine, from which they make a passable brandy. We remained for three days in this place.

To the Presidio of Guajoquilla.

On the 24th we traveled fourteen leagues, taking a general route northeast over level land well-wooded with low mesquites and huizaches. At the end of eight leagues there is the pueblo and mission Atotonilco on the bank of the Florido river. It is inhabited by 300 Tarahumares Indians and administered by a Franciscan friar. They live on maize and wheat, of which they harvest as much as 2,000 bushels, and some wine.

This presidio was erected under the name of Nuestra Señora de las Caldas de Guajoquilla during the viceroyship of his Excellency the Count of Revilla Gigedo. The work was begun on the first of June, 1752. Its company was composed of sixty-six men, including captain, lieutenant, and ensign. Its allowance amounted to 24,300 pesos annually. But this number of men was reduced to forty, twenty-six men having been taken away, including the lieutenant, for the formation of the new presidio of San Buenaventura valley, which was established at the beginning of the year 1766. There are also thirty-one settlers, who, with their families, amount to 195 persons. We were detained there until the seventh of the following month to review this presidio. During this time I made a plan of it, and after taking observations I found it to be in 27°50' north latitude, and in 261°30' longitude. We also went out and examined the surroundings on the 2nd of June, returning on the 3rd.

On this trip we traveled thirty leagues, of which I made a sketch wherein are shown the principal entrances of the enemies.

JUNE

To the Hacienda of San Antonio de la Ramada.

On the 7th we traveled ten leagues approximately north, over a plain wooded with many low mesquites, huizaches, etc. At one league we crossed the Florido river, which has very little water, and often dries up entirely. Its course, outlined by many poplar trees, turns to the right and winds around the foot of the very rugged and precipitous Chupaderos sierra, whose summit is impassable. Behind this chain, which is very high, and parallel to it the peaks of another chain could be seen. Between the two is a valley. A number of other mountains were also noted in the same direction. We stopped at the San Antonio de Ramada hacienda, which has several small adobe houses forming a square with circular towers. There are 210 persons in it engaged in mule breeding. Its products consist of 2,715 bushels of various kinds of grain which is their usual harvest. Because of its good and abundant pasture large numbers of horses and mules are raised.

To the Abandoned Presidio of Conchos or Pueblo of Nuestra Señora de Guadalupe.

On the 8th we traveled twelve leagues to the west over ground like the preceding. At the end of four leagues is the hacienda Nuestra Señora de Aranzazú. Three leagues from this is the pueblo and mission of San Francisco, inhabited by two hundred Chizos and Tarahumares Indians and administered by a Franciscan friar. One league farther on is the abandoned San Francisco de Conchos presidio. Adjoining it a small pueblo named Nuestra Señora de

Guadalupe has grown up and has a white population of twenty-five families. They maintain themselves very meagerly by weaving cloth, which is their principal occupation. This place is on the bank of the Conchos river, which flows in a very wide bed, and is so deep that it is impossible to irrigate this land.

To Chancaple.

On the 9th we traveled fourteen leagues on a general course north-northwest over a plain which ended in several hills situated in a circle and thickly wooded with mesquite, etc. At the start we forded the Conchos river in shallow water. There is nothing of interest until arriving at Chancaple, which is reduced to two or three abandoned huts on account of fear of Indian enemies. It has a very scanty water supply.

To the Hacienda of San Lucas.

On the 10th we traveled thirteen leagues on a general course west-northwest over ground similar to the preceding with the exception of some small hills. We stopped at the San Lucas hacienda on the left bank of the San Pedro river which we crossed in shallow water. There is an abundance of grain and the country is very pleasant. The soil has been fertilized through irrigation by a flume which brings water from the river.

One league up the river is the pueblo and mission of San Pedro, inhabited by Conchos Indians, not of the best reputation. Near it there is also the Santa Cruz pueblo. Both are administered by a Franciscan friar. There is no water in this whole journey.

To La Pastoria de Mapula.

On the 11th we traveled sixteen leagues northwest. There was no water in this stretch except for a single well which had very little. The ground was like that of the pre-ceding day. We stopped at a small sheep ranch called Mapula, consisting of a few huts. Here we found some thirty persons employed in cattle herding under contract with Chihuahua.

In these last two or three days' journey there is a good deal of danger and one must travel with great caution. Enemies commit outrages upon travelers every day, taking advantage of the rugged nature of the surrounding moun-tains to escape pursuit. Everywhere in these hills there are silver mines which have not been worked for fear of the barbarians. Near Mapula there is a small stream. It has very little water, for the whole section is very dry. This sheep ranch is somewhat isolated on the left side of the highway.

To the Town of Chihuahua.

On the 12th we traveled six leagues northwest. The road is good except for one stretch of loose rock. It passes through a little valley one league wide which is very dan-gerous, as it is infested by Indians. At the end there is a small pass with a gentle rise, and then one enters a great grassy plain called El Bajío from which the enemies have carried off many horses. Then, after passing over some gentle rolling hills covered with small stones, one arrives at Chihuahua.

This town is situated on arid ground on the bank of a small shallow stream. It is in 28°56' north latitude and 261°55' longitude. Its population consists of four hundred families of Spaniards, mestizos, and mulattoes, who are perishing because of the total failure of the mines and the constant hostilities of the Indians who have stolen all the mules and horses and have killed many persons in the neighborhood. A quarter of a league up the river is the church of Nuestra Señora de Guadalupe. Around it a small settlement of some thirty Yaqui Indians has grown up. On the opposite side are the mission and the Indian pueblo of Nombre de Dios, situated in a very pleasant valley, well cultivated, where they harvest all kinds of grain and a variety of fruits. This valley is formed by hills on the left side and on the right by a chain of very high mountains, precipitous in parts, where there are several gold mines unworked because the metal is insufficient. A creek passes through it which unites with the Chihuahua near the town. In this place there is a corregidor, and a parish priest who ministers to the people. Because of the scarcity of pasture on the trip our animals arrived in a useless condition and we remained here from the 12th of June until the 7th of July to replenish our supplies and rest our animals.

JULY

To the Mission of San Gerónimo.

On the seventh we traveled seven leagues north, one quarter northeast, the first six leagues over El Bajío plain until we came to the Chihuahua river ford. On our left, at a distance of a league or two, was the place called Tabalaopa where the Jesuits held a large hacienda. Five leagues on the right, in a chain of very rugged mountains which have given a great deal of silver, was the mining town of Santa Eulalia. At present, however, very little silver is being taken out. At the foot of this chain is the Chinarras mission, inhabited by Conchos Indians, administered by a Jesuit. Half a league from the ford is Santa Ana mission, and following it a little valley 400 *toesas* [852 yards] wide at its entrance, through which the Chihuahua river runs. Then comes the San Gerónimo mission of Tarahumares Indians, administered by a Franciscan friar. It is half a league from the first-mentioned, which used to have a Jesuit minister.

To Palo Blanco.

On the 8th we traveled eight leagues north through a wide valley, formed by the San Gerónimo mountains on the left and on the right the Realito de Santa Eulalia sierras, to the Palo Blanco hacienda. The latter has been abandoned out of fear of the Indians. In it there is a very scanty spring, but on the road there is no water whatsoever. In the San Gerónimo mountains there are several passes frequented by the enemies in their forays to Chihuahua.

To the Hacienda de Hormigas.

On the 9th we traveled eight leagues northeast. Four of them passed through the valley of the previous day where the two chains forming it draw close together and leave an opening or pass of 400 *toesas*. It is called El Puerto de Hormigas. From there one crosses over small hills until arriving at the hacienda of the same name. We found it abandoned. It has a spring with plenty of water and a large pond where cattle drink. There is a large number of these cattle, which have no watering place anywhere else, nor is there one on the entire road.

The San Gerónimo mountains end four leagues from this hacienda in a wide valley where one sees on the left Encinillas and on the right Julimes and the confluence of the Conchos and Norte rivers. We were going to review the presidio situated there. That night we learned that the governor of Nueva Vizcaya, to whom powers had been given to improve its location, had ordered it removed immediately to Julimes el Viejo. It was therefore necessary for us to change our direction to El Paso del Río del Norte, thus wasting all the effort of the previous journeys.

In Uninhabited Country.

On the 10th we left at noon, after watering the mules, for there was no water on the road until reaching Agua Nueva. We traveled eight leagues to the northwest over several plains ending in mountains forming an approximate circle. The pass from one to the other is through low hills and an occasional little valley. This night we slept in the field where there was no lack of pasture, but no water.

To Los Reyes, Uninhabited.

On the 11th we traveled ten leagues in the same direction over level ground as far as Los Reyes, near the San Bernardo spring. This spring is a short distance to the right of the highway by which one may also travel to the Agua Nueva hacienda, three leagues from each of the places above named. This country is composed of many hills of different heights and ruggedness forming a narrow ravine through which the road leads to a small pass. From this pass the hacienda at the foot of the slope may be seen. It is in a valley which could be very pleasant with its abundance of water if the enemies would permit its cultivation. We found three or four servants at this hacienda who were caring for a small town which owes its existence to the fact that it is surrounded by an adobe wall. This wall has circular towers, where those unfortunate people always keep a sentinel posted in order not to be in danger of losing their heads at any moment. On an aqueduct which comes from a spring near the hacienda is a flour mill. It is not now in use because it cannot be approached where it is situated without great danger.

This country is all hills and mountains and thus affords great facilities to the enemy to watch for favorable opportunities to attack the hacienda and then offers them a refuge to which they can retreat. A company of fifty sol-

diers destined for the presidio of La Junta de los Ríos had
been left temporarily at Agua Nueva, but the place was of
so little advantage to us they destroyed it when they left.
Despite this action, a council held by the governor of the
province of Chihuahua and some of its captains decided,
after too little consideration and even less knowledge of
the terrain, to station a detachment of thirty men and an
officer there. This was done after we passed through, but
in a short time the enemy stole all their horses, killed and
wounded several of the men, and, being emboldened by
this success, are daily inflicting injuries upon them. The
maintenance of this post offers no protection to the province. It is in fact experiencing double losses since the removal of the presidio from Junta, commonly called Del
Norte, and its establishment at Julimes el Viejo. The latter is there suffering the same occurrences as have taken
place at Agua Nueva. The men have been left on foot
repeatedly through loss of horses and, in consequence, are
helpless to defend themselves.

To the Spring of El Chivato.

On the 12th we continued nine leagues to the north-
northwest over level ground with good pasture and no
other markings than a little brush. There are several hills
in sight, among them that of Los Arados, at whose foot is
the Chivato waterhole where we camped. Because of its
rugged nature this range is the usual fortress of the enemies and serves them as a retreat in their forays. For this
reason the spring is very dangerous, as is that of Gallego,
which lies to the right of the road among some hills midway on this day's journey. They are favorite meeting
places of the Apaches, who by agreement divide themselves into several groups, some taking the valley which
leads to Encinillas lagoon, others that of Santa Clara
valley, and others going by way of Hormigas. They make

their way into Chihuahua and its vicinity, and after attacking in several places they meet by prearrangement at the aforesaid mountains and springs. Then, taking the road to Gila by way of the Cerro del Chile or the Sierra Blanca, and that of Siete Ríos by way of Agua Amargosa, the plains of Los Castillos and San Elceario, they return to their rancherías safely. They always find shelter in the continuous mountain ranges as is shown on the general map where they are all delineated.

To the Waterhole of Jesús María.

Four leagues from the Agua Nueva hacienda we came out on the highway which goes straight from Chihuahua through Encinillas to El Paso del Río del Norte. Traveling from La Junta to this place we made a round-about trip of many leagues.

On the 13th we traveled eight leagues north one quarter northwest over ground like the preceding. There were similar mountain ranges with a wide intervening valley. We camped at the small waterhole of Jesús María, a tiny pond of rain water caught in a little ravine at the foot of a very steep hill. It is near a small pass. To the east of this lies the valley of Santa Clara, now abandoned and overrun by enemies.

To Ojo Caliente and Carrizal.

On the 14th we traveled nine leagues north, one quarter northwest and northwest over ground like the preceding. At three leagues we crossed dry-shod over the Carmen river. East of it, at the foot of a small hill, is a very copious hot spring. Here there are ruins of a fine hacienda, once known as Ojo Caliente, and it is here that the jurisdiction of New Mexico begins. The place is five leagues from the small settlement of Carrizal, where we spent the night.

DESCRIPTION OF NUEVA VIZCAYA

Before entering the district of New Mexico, it will be advisable to give a general idea of the province of Nueva Vizcaya, describing in detail the frontiers subject to hostilities, since that is the principal object of my commission.

This extensive province lies between 23° and 33° north latitude, and between 255° and 271° longitude, west of the Tenerife meridian. It is bounded by Nayarit, Nueva Galicia, Costa del Real, and Minas del Rosario, which belong to its jurisdiction, and by the provinces of Culiacán, Sinaloa, Ostimuri, and Sonora. It embraces the whole of Tarahumara Alta situated in the Sierra Madre, as far as the pueblos of Maicoba, Yepomera, Totoaca, subject to the government of Sonora, and the province of Gila, inhabited by the Gileños Apaches or Chafalotes. It is also bounded by New Mexico, the province of Coahuila, and the New Kingdom of León. These provinces, in the order named, encircle it, beginning on the south and making a turn to the west, as is shown in considerable detail on the general map. The map also includes the subdivision of this province and those of Tepehuana, Tarahumara, Topia, and Batopilas, included in the area between the two Sierra Madres extending from southeast to northwest.

The Indian nations inhabiting these provinces are the Xiximes, Tubares, Berroxios, Xixies, Tarahumares, Nuris, Tepehuanes, Baborigames, Arapabondas, Conchos, Chizos, Otaquitatomes, Sumas, Xocomes, Mesquites, Cacalotes, Paxalames, Mammetas, Julimes, Tapalcomes, Poarames, Hopomes, Sibulos, Pulicas, and Sisimbres; but the greater part are included under the name of Tepehuanes and Tarahumares, divided into various pueblos

75

and administered by Franciscan fathers and some parish priests.

The principal towns of Spaniards, mestizos, and mulattoes are Durango, the capital, Saltillo, the pueblo of Parras, the mining town of Parral, San Bartolomé valley, the presidios of El Pasaje, Cerro Gordo, Guajoquilla, Junta de los Ríos, San Buenaventura valley and Janos valley, San Phelipe or mining town of Chihuahua, the town of El Nombre de Dios, and the mining town of Cosiguarichi. There are many haciendas in these territories, the number of whose inhabitants I could not ascertain because no one takes the trouble to keep account of them.

This province enjoys a mild climate. It produces many Spanish fruits, particularly the grape at Parras, Saltillo, San Bartolomé valley, and Durango. Generally water is very scarce. For this reason much of the land is uncultivated and uninhabited and serves only in some places for raising mules, horses, and cattle of all kinds. The region would be entirely covered with them if the enemies did not drive them off. There is scarcely a mountain range without gold and silver mines of more or less value.

The Apache Indians are the only ones who commit hostilities against this province. They are situated along its entire frontier from the province of Coahuila to Sonora. Beginning with Coahuila, the principal entrances used by them are as follows: the pass of Sobaco de Don Bartolomé near Parras; the Sardinas pass, near the Laguna de Parras; Tagualilo pass; Tianguis, facing Mapimí; from the latter to Banderas, which is also near by; from Banderas to the small hills of Upa, near La Cadena; from here to Pozo Hediondo, near Pelayo and El Gallo; the pass through the Conejitos mountains, near La Boca de Cerro Gordo; from this to Los Remedios near Guajoquilla; by the passes of Las Cañas, Batuecas, and Chupaderos, all in the Barrasas mountains, as is shown on the

map I mentioned when discussing the vicinity of the last
named presidio; through Terrazas, near the Conchos hot
spring, and from it to El Chiquazo, called the Puerto
Grande, from which they go to El Ancón de Carros. They
also enter this place by the sierra of El Agua Enterrada.
By way of La Tinaja they come out at La Boquilla de
Julimes; from the latter to Chorreras, El Infierno hill, and
San Diego hill; by Morrión pass to Dolores, or to Hormigas pass; from here to La Peña Blanca; from the latter to
El Venado. All of these passes lead to Nogal and from
there the greatest injuries have been inflicted on Chi-
huahua. The Apaches also come by way of the sierra of
Encinillas to Cueva pass. By Mala Noche they reach the
San Andrés sierra, and by Bilches they arrive at the
pueblo of the same name; by La Quemada they come to
Don Antonio del Castillo lagoon and several other places
which they visit less frequently.

The entrances most commonly used by the Lipán
Apaches are those situated between Coahuila and Julimes.
These Indians, although they are at peace with the provinces of Coahuila and Texas, constantly attack Nueva
Vizcaya, sometimes separately and sometimes joined by
the Natages. They come by way of that uninhabited section which could be cut off immediately, as well as all those
avenues of entrance, by advancing the Guajoquilla presidio
to the banks of the Río Grande. The report which I sent
from Chihuahua on July 2, 1766, extensively demonstrates
the utility of this presidio, as does the map which accom-
panies it. Also, many other entrances could be avoided by
locating the presidios as indicated on the map and by
establishing the method of making war as prescribed.

The attacks of the Pharaones Apaches, either from
Sierra Blanca or Siete Ríos, occur in the neighborhood of
the presidio of El Paso del Norte. The Indians come over
the plains of Los Castillos, San Elceario, and Agua

Amargosa. These entrances are also used by the Natages
and Gileño Apaches when it suits them. But the principal
entrances of the last named are by way of the San Joaquín
trail west and north from San Buenaventura; by Casas
Grandes pass farther north, passing Janos presidio on the
right and reconnoitering at the Santa María river; through
Miguel pass farther north along the promontory of La
Escondida sierra; through Las Minas pass due north to
the beginning of the sierra La Escondida; through Ruiz
valley north and east; over the Cerro del Chile, to the
east; by the sierra of Los Arados, and through the Santa
Clara valley in the same direction, the latter to the south.
It is to be observed that all these attacks could be prevented if the presidios of Janos and Paso del Río del Norte
did their duty, for the places mentioned are behind them,
as also are the sierras of La Magdalena, La Candelaria,
La Mojina, and others where the enemies take shelter,
and from which they sally forth to attack haciendas and
travelers.

The two presidios of El Paso and Janos are perfectly
situated to make war on the Gileños, commonly known by
the name of Chafalotes. They are so-called for their former captain, who, although no longer able to go to war
because of his age, has retained command of the principal
rancherías. His three sons, Natenejui, Asquelile, and
Brazo Quebrado, live separately and wander about sub-
sisting by hunting and gathering mescal through the
sierras of El Hacha, La Boca, El Alamillo, San Policarpo,
La Florida, El Tabaco, Corral de Piedras, El Quinteros,
Santo Domingo, El Capulín, La Escondida, and the other
intervening hills and rugged mountains. There are also
other less notable chiefs with whom they unite to make
forays and commit robberies; afterwards they divide the
spoils. All those Indians are in the neighborhood of the
presidio of Janos, and their rancherías encircle it especially

in winter when extreme cold forces them to abandon the sierras of El Cobre and Los Mimbres. There are also other Indians from the more northerly Gila. This group maintains a sort of capital in Los Mimbres mountains where their chief, Chafalote, stays with many families and horses as long as the season allows. The horses are kept in a pasture or guarded in a place naturally enclosed. There are always a great many armed warriors.

The Apaches are a single nation, but are under the different names of Gileños, Carlanes, Chilpaines, Xicarillas, Pharaones, Mezcaleros, Natages, Lipanes, etc. These groups differ little in language and not at all in their arms which are bows and arrows. Neither do they differ in the extreme cruelty toward the conquered. They tear off their living flesh and eat it. They shoot arrows into them and, in short, inflict every imaginable cruelty upon them. Often in Nueva Vizcaya they have cut open living pregnant women and after taking out the infants beat them together until both were dead. They are extremely indolent and plant little or nothing. Thus they are compelled to steal their food.

A piece of mule, horse, or deer is all the same to them, but they prefer to steal mules and horses from the Spaniards, thereby assuring themselves of abundant food with less work than hunting. For this reason they always have been, are, and will be dangerous to their neighbors, whether at war or peace. To the shame and dishonor of the Spaniards, the provinces of Coahuila and Texas suffer daily at the hands of the Apaches. Although these provinces are friendly to the Lipanes, they receive from them a thousand injuries, which are gradually bringing their unhappy subjects to ruin.

The Apaches habitually go naked, with only a breech-clout. When they are going to war they paint their bodies and faces with many different colors made from several kinds of herbs. They call this "painting red." They adorn their heads with bonnets trimmed with feathers in different ways. Sometimes they add small horns, head bands, and other decorations, all for the purpose of terrifying their enemies. When they wish to put on gala dress in their rancherías or come to the Spanish towns, they wear a jacket with sleeves reaching to the wrists, ordinary trousers, stockings, and shoes made of buckskin sewn with great neatness. For this purpose the women prepare and skillfully work the skins which the men obtain in hunting. With them they make leggings reaching half-way up the leg, and to them they add a buckskin sole, thus making a shoe and stocking in one piece. Some use another skin to cover their bodies, but ordinarily they wear only the breechclout.

JURISDICTION OF NEW MEXICO

On the 14th, as I have already said, we arrived at Carrizal, a small settlement of mestizos and mulattoes. Although it was founded seven years ago it has had no increase in that time because it is continually exposed to Indian incursions, which do not permit the inhabitants to prosper. The abundant land and water would be sufficient for a great number of inhabitants, but no one desires to live in this country because of the great danger, for it is the pass by which enemy Gileños and Pharaones enter Nueva Vizcaya. A squad of ten men and a corporal from the presidio of El Paso is maintained at this place. However, since most of them are occupied in caring for their horses, they are of little or no use in guarding the settlement nor attacking the enemies who pass by daily with their spoils.

On the 15th we did not travel.

To the Spring of Lucero.

On the 16th we marched eight leagues to the north-northeast over level bare land, very marshy in rainy season. At the end of four leagues there is a very abundant spring near the medium-sized Los Platos [Patos] lagoon. At the end of another four leagues is Lucero spring with oily and salty water. Here we camped. This afternoon we had a furious rain storm with thunder and lightning. The lightning struck nearby and the wind was so strong that it blew down our tents, leaving us exposed throughout the downpour.

To the Pass of El Bordo.

On the 17th we traveled nine leagues taking a general course north one quarter northeast over a great plain with an abundance of pasture and here and there mesquite and huizaches. To the right were the Ranchería mountains midway to the Río Grande del Norte which is about three or four leagues the other side of them. On the left is La Candelaria of which I have already spoken. We went to camp near a small pool of very bad rain-water in El Bordo pass.

To an Uninhabited Place without Water.

On the 18th we traveled eleven leagues to the north. As soon as we crossed the little Bordo pass we entered some very troublesome sand dunes two leagues long with several slopes. These are formed either from the sands of the Río del Norte by the furious winds in these parts or super-imposed upon a small chain of hills already there. The sand dunes run approximately northwest for a distance of sixty leagues as far as the little San Francisco springs in the Gila province. One league after we had crossed them we came to another very sandy slope. Then we descended to a plain covered with mesquite, huizaches, etc. and traveled one league to the Samalayuca spring, which forms a pond surrounded by trees. It is necessary to approach cautiously, for enemies use it, and, from the shelter of its thickly wooded banks, are wont to surprise and kill passers-by. Seven leagues from this waterhole we camped at an uninhabited waterless place.

To the Presidio of El Paso del Norte.

On the 19th we traveled five leagues north over rolling hills with several small ravines and gorges along the road and much mesquite but little pasture. We arrived at the presidio of Nuestra Señora del Pilar del Paso del Río del Norte, where there is a cavalry company composed of forty-six men, one sergeant, and three officers. The annual cost of the company is 20,265 pesos.

The map I drew shows the arrangement of what they call a presidio and part of Guadalupe pueblo. Following the river to the east along its right bank one comes to the pueblos of San Lorenzo del Real, San Antonio de Senecú, San Antonio de La Isleta, La Purísima Concepción del Socorro, and the hacienda Los Tiburcios. These places constitute a continuous settlement seven leagues long. The inhabitants of Nuestra Señora de Guadalupe are Spaniards, mestizos, mulattoes, and Indians of the Tigua and Piro nations, and some Genízaros. At San Lorenzo are the Sumas Indians; at Senecú the Piros; at La Isleta the Tiguas; at Socorro more Piros. In each one there are a few civilized people. Those who live in Los Tiburcios hacienda belong to this class. The total is 5,000 souls.

All this stretch of land is very well cultivated, producing everything that is planted, particularly very good grapes which are in no way inferior to those of Spain. There are many European fruits which are produced in such abundance that they are allowed to rot on the trees. The inhabitants make passable wine and better brandy, but at times they do not harvest enough maize for their support, because the ground is devoted to vines and other crops.

The captain of the company is also the alcalde mayor, and the people are administered by five Franciscan friars who attend the five missions, each with a stipend of four hundred pesos annually, paid by his Majesty. These stipends could be saved by placing there one or two curates with assistants. This saving would be by no means small considering that the fertility of the country brings the missionary of Guadalupe alone an annual income of four hundred pesos.

When the first Spanish troops arrived here this country belonged to a peaceful nation which received them kindly. Because of this they were called Mansos. However, at the time of the second conquest of this kingdom, they were almost extinct and several colonies from the interior were moved in to repopulate this fertile piece of land. The place is situated, according to my observations, in 33°6' north latitude, and in 261°40' longitude, by the Tenerife meridian.

AUGUST

To El Ancón de la Cruz.

Having finished the review, we set out on the 5th. After crossing the Río Grande del Norte on rafts at the place called El Vado de Balisan, we traveled along the river bank over broken, well-wooded hills a distance of six leagues north-northwest. We halted at El Ancón de la Cruz de Juan Téllez, having on the right the so-called sierra of La Otra Banda or Los Mansos. This range extends east to west until it reaches this place. Then it bears southeast to a valley and afterwards takes a northerly direction.

To the Uninhabited Place of Los Cacaxtitos.

On the 6th we traveled six leagues north over level ground with some ravines. On our left for a distance of not more than a league the river was thickly wooded. On our right, for three or four leagues, was the sierra of Los Mansos, commonly called Los Órganos because of irregular peaks in this chain which resemble pipes of an organ. We camped at Los Cacaxtitos near the river. One league from this place, bearing northeast one quarter north, is Los Alamitos pass in the sierra of Los Órganos.

Through Unpopulated Country to Los Bracitos.

On the 7th we traveled eight leagues to the northwest over level ground like the preceding. Between the river which flows a short distance away and the sierra of Los Órganos there is a space of one league. In the sierra are several passes formed by rolling hills. The rest of the range is very high and rugged. We stopped to camp on the bank of the river at Los Bracitos. Three leagues east of this place is Los Órganos pass. From there the sierra takes a northwesterly direction. To the east-northeast there is a valley which, turning again to the east, leads to the Soledad spring situated in the center of that valley at a distance of eight or nine leagues. Some Apache rancherías are permanently located there, as well as at San Agustín spring ten or twelve leagues to the north-northeast on the other side of some peaks. To the north is the San Nicolás range, fourteen to sixteen leagues distant.

Through Uninhabited Country to El Ancón de Roblerito.

On the 8th we traveled nine leagues in the same direction over land like the preceding but with woods of mesquite, huizache, etc., so thick that the vehicles had great difficulty in passing through. On our right we had the Doña Ana range; on our left, the river in a serpentine course. The widest turns are a league apart. This interval is composed of some hills which continue to rise toward the sierra. The Doña Ana range runs from south to north for about four leagues bearing to the east of El Ancón de Roblerito, where we camped on the river bank. To the north is the Roblero sierra, a small range of hills running to the northwest and terminating in some isolated flat-topped rocks. At its foot the river flows along for two leagues to the southwest. On the other side of the river is the Roblerito sierra, very high and rugged, running in the

same direction for four leagues. Across the river are some
very large pasture lands generally inhabited by Apaches.
Their proximity, and the shelter afforded the Indians by a
labyrinth of hills, make this pass very dangerous. It is here
that travelers are commonly attacked.

To Perrillo, an Uninhabited Place.

On the 9th we traveled ten leagues north-northwest
over level ground with little undergrowth or pasture.
There are many wild palms producing very good dates
different in shape and taste from those of Spain. After
traveling four leagues, we saw, two leagues west of the
road, the San Diego sierra on the river's edge. Here a halt
is usually made because at this point begins the Jornada
del Muerto where there is seldom any water. Thus water
is generally taken on here. After the mules have drunk,
travelers set out on the road, starting in the evening to
take advantage of the night's coolness. They travel two
nights, one day and part of another without stopping in
order to reach Fray Cristóbal. The river is encountered
again after thirty leagues. We passed San Diego on the
left, and set out for El Perrillo. We camped on the edge
of a ditch where there was a little rainwater. On our right
and continuing north was the sierra of Los Órganos. On
the left El Perrillo sierra, extending in the same direction
and meeting the very high and rugged El Muerto. At the
foot on the other side the river becomes very deep and
narrow. Although it is possible for the animals to go down
to drink, it is seldom done because of the round-about trip,
the long steep descent, and the great danger from Apaches
who always live in that vicinity and often pass by.

To the Lake of El Muerto, Uninhabited.

On the 10th we traveled fourteen leagues to the north
over ground like the preceding. At the end of six leagues is

El Alemán, where there is usually some rainwater collected in several pools, but we found them dry. Eight leagues farther on is El Muerto lagoon. We camped there although it was dry.

To Fray Cristóbal, Uninhabited.

On the 11th we traveled ten leagues northeast, the first five as far as the summit of San Cristóbal sierra. The sierra turns northwest and so does the road for four leagues. Then the road turns north for a league to Fray Cristóbal. We camped there on the bank of the river. For five leagues from the summit of the sierra the ground varies and is composed of hills and rocks.

The scarcity of water might be avoided by traveling along the opposite bank of the river, which is supposed to be accessible, even though it is winding, and withdraws as much as ten leagues from the road. Our road was selected because it is shorter and because it extends through the middle of the plain where Indians cannot attack travelers so easily. Nevertheless, on the night of the 9th and the 10th they surrounded our horses at Perrillo, watching for an opportunity to steal them; but, having been perceived by a soldier who was going the rounds, they changed their minds and retired. On the following day hostile Indians attacked ten Sumas Indians who, contrary to orders, had gone ahead with some sheep we were taking for provisions. Some of them resisted, but others were driven toward El Perrillo sierra. When the news reached the camp the attackers were pursued and some of the prey recovered. They had been killing the sheep with lances and arrows whenever they found it necessary to abandon them.

At the same time other Indians came out of El Perrillo hills where they were in ambush and attempted to attack the cordon, expecting to find it off guard. Although this was indeed the case, and there were not enough men to defend it if it had been strongly attacked, a halt was made to await the Indians. This discouraged them, and, contenting themselves with skirmishing around outside the range of guns, they went off to join thirty or forty others who could be seen on horseback drawn up in a row on the ridge of the hills. All the rest of that day they paralleled us on our right.

To the Wood of the Apache, Uninhabited.

On the 12th we traveled twelve leagues northeast. At one league is the dangerous pass called El Contadero, extending three leagues over hills and hollows, forming a bad defile to the Senecú mesa. For this reason we reconnoitered before entering with the vehicles. Here we saw ruins of the Senecú pueblo, which was abandoned on the second entrance of the Spaniards into this kingdom. Two leagues farther, on the bank of the river, is San Pascual. The remaining six leagues lead us to the Apache woods where we camped near the river. These places are equally hilly. Along the road there is plenty of pasture.

To the left, on the other side of the river, is the very rugged and high central range called Los Ladrones, which joins the Mimbres range. The chain continues as far as Sonora. To the right, in the distance, the sierra of Los Órganos and several of its passes are visible.

To the Abandoned Pueblo of Alamillo.

On the 13th we traveled thirteen leagues northeast following the course of the river. The first four leagues were over swampy ground with a great deal of coarse grass and reeds up to the ruins of Luis López' houses, which are to be seen on both banks. In front of those on this side there is a good stretch of road through a valley where the *vueltas* of Acumilla or Luis López begin. These are several fairly high hills, with many steep slopes. In some places the vehicles are very much in danger of going over the edge. These *vueltas* extend over a space of three leagues. Before leaving this stretch one sees on the opposite side of the river the ruins of Socorro pueblo, at the foot of the Socorro sierra, which runs at a high elevation in front of Los Ladrones sierra. The remaining three leagues are over level road with an occasional ravine and finally terminate at the ruins of Alamillo pueblo, on the left bank of the river. We camped there. During the whole day we had the chain of Los Órganos some distance away on our right. Between it and the river there are many rolling hills.

To the Pueblo of Bethlem.

On the 14th we traveled fourteen leagues north with some deviations northeast, over hills with steep descents. The first four leagues brought us to the ruins of the Sevilleta pueblo, on the left bank of the river. Opposite is the junction of the Puerco river, whose waters always flow muddy and turgid from its source in the Navajoó province. Four leagues farther on is the recently formed small settlement of Las Nutrias. Thirty families live there in huts made of skins. They have very few implements for cultivating the soil and fewer arms for their defense, notwithstanding that they are located in the midst of Apaches Gileños, and Pharaones. About halfway along this road are the ruins of the houses of Felipe Romero. From Las Nutrias to the pueblo of La Limpia Concepción, called Tomé, and also Fuenclara, it is six leagues by good level road in the same direction. The population consists of seventy Spanish residents. Opposite it, on the other side of the river, is the pueblo of Bethlem with thirty-eight families of Genízaros and Spaniards. In both places all kinds of grain abound, as well as sheep, and there is plenty of good pasture everywhere in the vicinity.

Five or six leagues from Alamillo, on the other side of

the river, the sierra Los Ladrones begins, and a little farther on El Socorro, while on the right Los Órganos continues.

On the 15th we did not travel.

To the Town of Alburquerque.

On the 16th we traveled ten leagues to the north with some deviations one quarter northeast, over a plain extensively forested with poplar trees along the river's edge. Halfway along this road, on the other side, is La Isleta pueblo of Tiguas Indians administered by a Franciscan friar. We halted at the town of Alburquerque, a settlement composed of seventy Spanish families. They have eighty militiamen, well mounted and armed, with their corresponding officers. They are administered by a curate who is a Franciscan friar.

To Sandía Mission.

On the 17th we traveled five leagues in the same direction over ground like the preceding. We halted at Sandía, inhabited by Tiguas and Moquinos Indians, who have the pueblo divided into two sections where the nations live separately. They are administered by a Franciscan friar. Just before reaching this mission Los Órganos, or Los Mansos sierra, ends.

To Santo Domingo Mission.

On the 18th we traveled eight leagues in the same direction over ground like the preceding. On both sides of the river there are several small ranches called Bernalillo. Four leagues from this place, on the right bank, is San Felipe mission, a Keres Indian pueblo, with ninety-five families, administered by a Franciscan friar. Just before this, on the same side, is the junction of the Santa Ana river. On its banks six leagues beyond Bernalillo are two pueblos of Keres Indians, Santa Ana and Sía, and the pueblo of Jemes inhabited by Indians of that name. Finally, two and a half leagues from San Felipe, is Santo Domingo, inhabited by eighty-eight families of the same Keres nation, also administered by a Franciscan friar.

To Santa Fé, the Capital.

On the 19th we traveled ten leagues, part of it southeast and afterwards to the east over low hills with some steep and very rocky ravines. Drawing away from the river which flows approximately north to south we arrived at Don Tenorio's hacienda after traveling six leagues. Four leagues over a better road brought us to the town of Santa Fé, capital of the Kingdom of New Mexico. By my observations, I found this town to be situated in 36° 10′ north latitude and 262° 40′ longitude.

The map I drew shows its layout. It also shows that its presidio is incapable of defense. Nevertheless a small fort would be a help for safe-guarding the families and properties in case of a general uprising. In this way the many disasters that occurred in the last outbreak — namely, the loss of the Kingdom, which was recovered at immense expense — could be avoided.

A company of eighty soldiers, including the lieutenant, ensign, and two sergeants, is maintained in this capital. This costs His Majesty 34,070 pesos annually.

The population amounts to 2,324 persons, divided among the eighty families of soldiers, 274 Spanish settlers, and 89 families from various Indian nations.

SEPTEMBER

Return to the Presidio of El Paso del Norte.

On the 15th we set out from the presidio of Santa Fé after concluding the review. Returning by the same road and passes over which we had come, we arrived on the 28th at El Paso. Nothing particular occurred in the hundred and twenty-two leagues of the journey.

OCTOBER

After being unavoidably detained in El Paso, we left there on the 8th. Retracing the road by which we had come from Carrizal, we arrived there on the 10th, having traveled thirty-three leagues. Shortly before our arrival some Natages Indians had passed through this vicinity with the horses they had just stolen from the detachment at Agua Nueva. In this encounter some soldiers were killed and wounded. On their retreat the Indians attacked the Carmen hacienda. They passed through Carrizal, the plain of Los Castillos, Agua Amargosa, and, fording the Río Grande del Norte, returned victorious to their homes.

It becomes necessary to speak again of Nueva Vizcaya, since our route passed through that district. Hence I shall first finish what I have to say regarding New Mexico.

DESCRIPTION OF THE KINGDOM OF
NEW MEXICO

It is situated between 32° and 38° north latitude, and between 258 and 264 degrees longitude, reckoning by the Tenerife Meridian. It has thirty-seven settlements as is indicated on the general map. In them live 2,703 families of Teguas, Genízaros, Tiguas, Abiquius, Pecuries, Taos, Pecos, Janos, Zuñis, Ácomas, Moquinos, Queres, Xemes, Sumas, and Piros Indians, making a total of 10,524 persons. The number of Spaniards comes to 9,580 persons, distributed among 1,487 families, the total amounting to 20,104 souls. The Indians as well as the Spaniards are well prepared for war, for they learn to use weapons and ride horses when they are very young. This they do in order to defend themselves against the heathen nations which surround them everywhere except to the south where they border on Nueva Vizcaya at Las Boquillas.

Indian arms are the bow and arrow, pikes or lances, and some guns. Many wear leather jackets. The arms of the Spaniards are the same as in the other provinces, the strongest being the lance, which they handle perfectly. They do not often use guns because of the scarcity of powder in that country and the fact that they are acquired at considerable cost and effort. Consequently they go on a campaign with little ammunition, thereby losing the advantage of fire-arms, the possession of which compensates for the disparity in number between our people and the Indians. At the present time the nations of the Navajos, Moquinos, Yutas, Apaches, Carlanes, and Chilpaines are at peace, and they are only troubled by the Apaches Gileños and Pharaones, whose locations are shown on the map.

They also suffer some small annoyances from the Comanche Indians, notwithstanding that they usually come to the annual fair at Taos. There they trade buckskins, buffalo hides, and slaves from various Indian nations situated to the east for clothing and horses. This nation is one of the most warlike. It is said that these Indians came from the north, following Las Grullas mountain chain and are known to our people as far as a hundred leagues above Mexico. According to reports they took six moons or months to reach our frontier, where, having been stopped by our forces, they turned east and established many rancherías on the banks of the Napestle river. Others wander about in the territory between this kingdom and San Sabá, extending as far as the Taguayas and Yscanís, where there are abundant buffalo. Buffalo are their principal food, together with certain fruits, similar to those of Europe, which grow naturally on the banks of the Napestle river. They live in tents or lodges made of buffalo hides. Their arms are the bow and arrow and a few guns acquired from the French, with whom they trade at a fort among the Taguayas. Sometimes the French come into their rancherías and live there for years.

New Mexico produces an abundance of every kind of grain, for its climate is very similar to that of Spain. There are many cattle and sheep and some ranches for horse breeding, which turn out extremely well. There is more than enough pasture, which is grama grass for the most part. The trading of the inhabitants is limited to a few buckskins or buffalo hides, which they bundle and take annually to Chihuahua. In return they bring clothing for their families. The Indians too are in the habit of going after clothing, but usually their women wear the cloth they themselves weave. They weave very good woolen cloth in attractive patterns. Skirts, blouses, and capes are made of this cloth. Their shoes consist of a sole fastened to the middle of a buckskin legging, which they wrap around the legs, making them look bulky as though they had on thick boots.

The men cover their bodies with buckskins, imitating to some extent Spanish dress. The inhabitants are also in the habit of taking some of their capes, stockings, and blankets to trade on the outside. They pay no attention to otter, beaver, ermines, and marten skins, which they have in abundance, because they do not know their value.

There are several rivers containing a large quantity of fish, particularly the Río Grande del Norte. The source of this river was unknown, although its banks have been explored as far as Las Grullas sierra, where it is supposed to have its source. The river could be used to build up a considerable trade with this province if the frontier were established on its borders and settled. The wines, brandy, grain, lumber, etc. of this province could be shipped by water to the new plantations. It could likewise carry to the Gulf of Mexico such surplus articles of trade as wool and hides, for this river is navigable in canoes for all this distance. This would produce admirable results and would greatly aid in making the new settlements an impenetrable barrier against the Indians who now enter through this uninhabited region to destroy our interior possessions.

In the mountains covered with oaks, pines, and large cedars are found buffalo, bears, wolves, coyotes, wild sheep, and also deer. Conspicuous among the last-named are the red deer, seven palms high, with horns two *varas* long from the roots to the tips. There is a great variety of birds. Partridges are abundant and are caught by hand after their first flight. There are also silver mines of no great value. They are not worked.

JURISDICTION OF NUEVA VIZCAYA

To the Carmen River.

On the 12th we traveled twelve long leagues to the south, one quarter southwest over level land covered with many mesquites, huizaches, and wild reeds. At two leagues, a short distance to the right of the road, is the ruined pueblo of Santa María. In its vicinity is a copious spring used for irrigation at Carrizal and conducted there by an aqueduct. One league to the north of the latter place is Santo Domingo canyon, also abandoned by the Sumas Indians who once lived there. The sierra of Los Arados, of which I have previously spoken, begins six leagues from Carrizal. Between this and a range of hills terminating in San Pedro pass the road runs through a valley. To the left is another valley leading to Encinillas lagoon. Both valleys are used by the enemies. At twelve leagues is the Carmen river with poplars along its banks. We forded it in shallow water and camped on the other side.

To the Hacienda of El Carmen.

On the 13th we traveled five leagues along the same route, two and a half of them through the valley of the preceding day as far as San Isidro pass. This pass is formed by a chain of low rolling hills. The river is avoided by making a turn of half a league to the right of the road and coming to an end in a cañon or opening in the said valley. After going through the pass, which is short, one descends to another plain. In this one the course of the river is indicated by the continuous growth of poplars on its banks. Among some hills a short distance from the river is the hacienda of El Carmen. Its owner, out of generosity and with considerable difficulty, supports 291 persons there. Among these are 35 men (Spaniards, I should say), armed with guns and arrows to defend themselves against the constant attacks of the enemies, who, despite precautions, have stolen many horses and killed many people.

To El Ojo Caliente.

On the 14th we traveled eight leagues west, with some deviations northwest. At five leagues is La Tinaja pass in some hills which run toward the Cerro del Chile. This pass is half a league long. Its passage is dangerous because it is the road used by the enemies. It is two and a half leagues from here to El Ojo Caliente where we camped. The spring is so-called because its water is quite warm. Eight *varas* from it is another cold water spring.

To San Buenaventura.

On the 15th we traveled four leagues west, the first league by a gentle slope with several ravines, some having water in them. There is a gradual ascent to the foot of the San Buenaventura pass, which is in a very high, rugged sierra. For its whole length of two leagues the road runs through a deep cañon, where a thousand tragedies are committed daily by the enemies. For this reason we took precaution to reconnoiter and take observations from the summits before sending the horses and loads into the defile. There is very little pasture in the country, except for an abundance of reed grass, which the animals cannot eat. There are mesquites, cat's claws and some cottonwoods at the waterholes. Once through the pass, one enters the San Buenaventura valley. At one league is the settlement situated in 30°16′ north latitude and 259°55′ longitude, reckoning by the Tenerife meridian.

The valley runs from south to north as far as the Miguel valley, sixteen leagues away. Its width from east to west is eight leagues from the Cerro Grande to the San Joaquín valley. The houses are scattered over an extent of about two leagues. Among its inhabitants may be counted the forty armed men of the newly-raised company which is kept provisionally in this place together with fifty-one soldiers, including three officers and a sergeant and costing 20,770 pesos annually.

The adobe houses of the pueblo where the company is stationed form an enclosure. Outside it there are many others, constructed wherever convenient. For this reason robberies and other outrages are committed at night.

To the River of Santa María.

On the 27th we traveled eight leagues, principally northwest, down the valley, along the river passing through it. At a distance of four leagues we found a ruined hacienda. Three leagues beyond, also abandoned, is the fort. There is a great deal of abandoned farm land here. One league from this we forded the Santa María river and camped on the other side. There are two chains of very high sierras which form San Buenaventura valley. They are San Miguel and San Buenaventura. San Miguel, on the left, is very precipitous in its entire length and permits passage only by way of the large hill, El Biscocho, the small valley of Doña Catharina and that of San Joaquín. It is seldom crossed by the Apaches who do not want to be obliged to take their plunder through any settled place and therefore always come through the San Buenaventura sierras on the right as they are more accessible.

To La Punta de los Alamos.

On the 28th we traveled fourteen leagues to the northwest over level land through the valley of the preceding day as far as the pueblo of El Chocolate, six leagues distant. This is an open pass, low and not at all dangerous, extending three leagues between hills until it comes out at Casas Grandes valley. The hills on the left are the continu-

ation of the San Miguel range, whose elevation decreases
very much here. The hills on the right are of the same
height, and behind them may be seen the very high and
rugged sierra La Escondida, inhabited by the enemies. At
the entrance of this valley is the small El Chocolate hill
after which the pass is named.

After leaving this pass it is three leagues to the river.
A quarter of a league after fording it one sees, on a small
elevation, the remains of a very old town, called Las Casas
Grandes de Moctezuma. Its ruins show it to have been of
several levels. On one side of the rectangle which is formed
by two plazas is a number of small rooms in two rows. According to their dimensions and measurements, they seem
to me to have been intended for wild animal cages. On the
other sides are fragments of walls several *varas* high and
constructed of blocks of earth three to five feet in thick-
ness, plastered in parts and whitewashed with a white
earth which the Spaniards in this country still use. From
this place it is three leagues to La Punta de los Alamos
where we camped on the left bank of the Casas Grandes
river. In the intervening space are a number of ruined
houses. Others are still standing but are abandoned because
of the constant hostilities of the Apaches who have destroyed the few settlers who lived in this pleasant valley.

To the Presidio of Janos.

On the 29th we traveled thirteen leagues north one quarter northwest by the valley of the preceding day. At seven
leagues is the Ramos pass where there are two canyons.
The first is formed by some very high hills and the sierras
of Las Bocas, through which the road passes. The other
lies between the opposite side of these sierras and that of
Capulin where the river enters and forms a small turn on
the right of the road. The first is called Ramos pass. It is
extremely dangerous and is full of crosses for the dead
who have been killed there by the enemies. It is two leagues

to the place where it again opens into the same Casas Grandes valley, which again widens and forms a plain covered with low woods. It terminates at a distance of four leagues in some hills. At the foot is the presidio of San Felipe y Santiago de Janos on a small elevation on the left bank of a creek of the same name. The latter flows northeast and empties into the Casas Grandes river two leagues lower down.

By the map I drew of this presidio the shape and arrangement of its enclosure can be seen. According to my observations, I found it to be situated in 31°18' north latitude and in 258°24' longitude. In it there is a cavalry company of fifty-one soldiers, including three officers, a first chaplain, and a sergeant, costing 20,670 pesos annually.

This settlement is composed of a hundred and one families of mestizos and mulattoes, including those of the company. In all there are 455 persons. Of these, thirty-seven armed men live outside the enclosure in small huts. Some of these huts are about to be abandoned because they are falling and in others open gaps show. Most of the houses in the settlement are uninhabitable, with the exception of the captain's which has been rebuilt.

NOVEMBER

To the Arroyo of La Palotada, Uninhabited.

We remained here for the purpose of reviewing the presidio until the 13th of this month when we set out to the north-northwest in search of the presidio of Fronteras. After traveling three leagues we halted and camped on the banks of La Palotada arroyo, which has its origin one league farther up in Los Sauces. Half a league from the presidio the Puerto Grande is formed by some hills. It is not very long, but is quite dangerous because of the enemies who lie in ambush there and unexpectedly attack travelers. At a considerable distance to the left one sees the Sierra Madre running from south to north and forming the boundary between this province and Sonora. Most prominent in this chain are the Carcay and Alisos sierras. On their slopes these ranges form a canyon where the little Janos river rises. In the immediate neighborhood is the Janos house, at present abandoned. Then follow the Carretas sierra and pass, through which one goes to Santa María Baseraca within the jurisdiction of Sonora, whose boundaries on this side include the Sierra Madre. The sierra of Enmedio can also be seen. Here there is no lack of rancherías notwithstanding that those acquainted with the country believe there is no water there. The belief may arise because they have not examined the interior thoroughly. At the right of the hill—I should say at the right of the pass—there are several difficult hills following the course of La Palotada arroyo and continuing by Ojo Caliente which is on its bank.

To San Francisco, Uninhabited.

On the 14th we traveled eleven leagues northwest through a spacious plain, broken by the Enmedio sierra and a chain of bare hills, which run, with several openings, from south to north. Between these hills and the Enmedio sierra the road passes near a small spring at the northern point of Enmedio sierra, nine leagues from our starting place, and two from San Francisco where we camped.

The plain traversed this day extends on the north from the Playa of Santo Domingo to Gila province; on the south to the Babicora plains; on the east the plain terminates in some mountain chains, especially noteworthy as shelter for the enemies. The same is to be said of those lying to the west according to the way I viewed them from San Francisco. In relation to the last-named place La Hacha hill extends north-northeast at a distance of twelve leagues.

Eight leagues northeast one quarter north is the Alamo Hueco. Six leagues north-northwest is Las Animas sierra whose chain terminates the plain on the north, one quarter to the northwest, where there are several valleys. Through them one may leave the plain. To the southeast is the northern point of Enmedio sierra.

To Los Chupaderitos, an Uninhabited Place.

On the 15th we traveled nine leagues, the first five north-northwest over level ground with abundant pasture. All the time we had Las Animas sierra in front of us which later we left to the right. Toward the northwest are some hills having many steep declivities, difficult for wagons. A league farther on one descends the Cañada de las Paces which is still another league in length. Then one enters San Luis plain between the sierra of the same name and that of Las Animas. We traveled through the last named plain two leagues south-southwest until we came to a spring and some *chupaderitos* where we camped. To the east was San Luis sierra and to the west the road to Fronteras; to the north San Simón pass, by which one also goes to Gila; to the north one quarter northwest, the sierra de Noche Buena; northwest, the Ciénega Fría; and west-southwest, the Cuchuberachi sierra; southwest, one quarter south the sierra Grande de Salsipuedes, on whose eastern point is the location of Babispe, mission of Opatas Indians, belonging to Sonora. The road from the latter to Fronteras follows along the foot of the northern ranges and terminates in the San Luis plain. The greatest width of this plain is, from south to north, twenty-six leagues, counting from the Salsipuedes sierra to San Simón pass, and from east to west it is six leagues wide. There is a great deal of good pasture in the plain and on the slopes, canyons, and wherever there is moisture. There are a good many red oaks.

JURISDICTION OF SONORA

To the Cañada of San Bernardino.

On the 16th we traveled fifteen leagues, the first five west through the San Luis plain where the jurisdiction of Sonora begins, to the hills by which one ascends to the cañada of Guadalupe. In that cañada the road is boxed in by several gorges, making many turns for the space of seven leagues, the principal direction being west-southwest, with many very dangerous precipices and cliffs. After traveling four leagues one comes to La Plazuela, a small plain surrounded by high mountains. Three leagues from it is the last slope, ending in a spacious mesa and stretching to the west, the direction we were following, for two leagues. The aforesaid cañada Guadalupe is formed by several ridges so steep that it appears impossible to cross them on wheels, although it is said that they have been crossed by some wheeled vehicles. At the bottom of the cañada is a small stream adorned with many poplars, and yews or alders. On the slopes and heights there are pines, oaks, mesquites, huizaches, and an infinite number of shrubs. Among them are many brown bear. One league from the mesa there is an arroyo in the Cañada de San Bernardino. After climbing several small hills in the stretch we camped in a little plain on the edge of this arroyo.

From the mesa one sees the Chiguicagui range twelve leagues to the north where the Apache rancherías have always been. These Indians keep up incessant hostilities against the province of Sonora. I shall speak of this more fully when I describe the province.

To La Tinaja Spring.

On the 17th we traveled twelve leagues south-southwest. The first seven by way of the San Bernardino valley, which is dangerous because of the cliffs, broken ground, and steep hills on both sides, as far as the small La Tinaja spring. This place is much used by the enemy in their incursions into Fronteras valley, especially by way of El Potrero nearby on the left. We followed this mountain chain to the Fronteras sierra nearby and opposite the presidio. The five remaining leagues are traveled to the south by La Tinaja canyon which was like Caguiona, the previous one. Here we camped on the banks of a stream.

To Fronteras or Presidio Corodeguachi.

On the 18th we traveled eight leagues, the first two over hills. On the last one there is a very steep slope descending to Fronteras valley. In that valley the land continues level with some small swamps caused by a spring. The latter is the source of the arroyo which runs to the foot of Caguiona and empties into the Fronteras river two leagues west of our camping place. Six leagues farther east is Corodeguachi presidio, otherwise known as Fronteras and situated according to my observation in 31°17′ north latitude and 255°24′ longitude, by the Pico de Theide meridian.

A sketch of the settlement and a part of its surroundings, which were surveyed very carefully, is shown on the map. Four hundred and seventy-nine persons live in it including a company of cavalry of fifty-one men, counting the three officers etc. Their allowance is the same as at the presidio of Janos. It has, in addition to the soldiers, fifty settlers skilled in the use of arms. In the country, which cannot be included in the map, there is to be noted to the east at a distance of one league, a very high rugged and overgrown hill commonly called Fronteras. From there the enemy is in the habit of spying upon whatever goes on at the presidio, for they can see even into its interior. At the foot of the hill is the Fronteras river, which forms a swamp in front of the settlement. Toward the west at a considerable distance is the Mababe range, famous for its many placers which have produced pure gold nuggets weighing from six to seven marks [48 to 56 ounces]. This tempting treasure, however, has cost the lives of many who went incautiously and unarmed to seek it.

DECEMBER

To Arroyo Hondo.

We remained in this presidio until the 4th of this month, when, having finished the review, we set out for the presidio of Terrenate, traveling eight leagues over well-pastured hills with water on all slopes. We made camp at the Arroyo Hondo, which is preceded by a very long descent. This stream, although it has very little water, is very rapid because of the depth of the canyon. On our left was the Mababe sierra terminating in the north at Magallanes pass, through which one may also go to Fronteras.

To El Paraje de Sauz.

On the 5th we traveled twelve leagues to the west. At half a league there is a slope, sharper and longer than that of the preceding day. It descends to a very deep canyon where the waterhole of El Gato is situated. Beyond this one reaches the more open Parida where there are many trees along the banks of the arroyo which comes from Magallanes sierra. At six leagues, counted from the beginning, the arroyo of Santa Bárbara joins the first-named through a canyon running from west to east and terminating at a hill. On the other side is the arroyo of León halfway between Fronteras and Terrenate. Finally, the road we followed, called El León, joins another coming through Magallanes pass at the arroyo of Los Nogales. This precedes by three leagues El Paraje de Sauz where we camped. Shortly before that, we had on our left Chiguicagui, the usual exit for the Tesocomachi or Mababe Indians. They go by way of Agua Verde from El Dado pass, situated at the northern point of this sierra. The whole of this stretch is hilly and pasture is unlimited.

To the Presidio of Terrenate or San Felipe de Jesús Guebabi.

On the 6th we traveled ten leagues west, the first five over gentle hills until we reached the source of the San Pedro river. This river rises in two adjoining springs on the left of the road and runs north to join the Gila in the Sobaipuris valley, also called San Pedro. Here are the ruins of the pueblos of Santa Cruz, Quibori, Tres Alamos, and Acequias Hondas. They were inhabited by the Sobaipuris Indians, who were compelled to abandon them because of constant robberies and murders committed by the Apaches from the shelter of the Chiguicagui sierra where they have never been pursued. In the said valley there is a great deal of farm land and plenty of water. We therefore preferred to pass through it to explore the Colorado river because the other attempted entrances were hindered by the arid Papaguería country, and by the immense waterless sand dunes on the southern bank. One league from the San Pedro river we crossed the Terrenate river at the place called Las Nutrias. The latter forms a lagoon one league above the said crossing. There the river resumes its course and gushes out again lower down. A creek coming from the northern part of Guachuca sierra three leagues away also empties into the lagoon. Here there are many silver mines producing very good ore. Beyond this lagoon is El Cabestro spring and following it a valley containing several swamps skirted by the two gentle ranges. We proceeded along the river's course as far as Terrenate presidio. According to my observation, the latter is situated in 31°35′ north latitude and 253°54′ longitude, by the Tenerife meridian.

The map I drew of this presidio, also called San Felipe de Jesús Guebabi, shows its situation, size, and arrangement. Its population consists of 300 persons including the company, which has the came complement of men as the two previously mentioned presidios. To this number may be added nineteen settlers skilled in the use of arms. Its climate is unhealthy and the water is not at all good, nor are there any farm lands nearby. For this reason, and despite the danger, settlers plant on the banks of the San Pedro river in the Sobaipuris valley, five leagues away. They maintain a storehouse there which has been burned two or three times by the enemy. This valley is very suitable for settlement and it would be well to move the presidio there so that settlers might gather under its protection. Undoubtedly they would be attracted by the good and abundant land there. In time this would facilitate and encourage work in the mines in the adjacent mountains, especially in the Guachuca mountains, which are now producing good silver, notwithstanding the scarcity of people and the excessive risk.

To San Antonio Pass.

We stayed until the 18th to review this company. Then we set out for the Tubac presidio, traveling nine leagues west-northwest over hills with plenty of pasture. Half a league farther one climbs the ridge of Las Bolas. Following the cañada Las Bolas five leagues from the presidio one comes to the source of a very small river named for Santa María Suamca, mission of the Pimas Altos. It is half a league away on the left of the road and was formerly administered by the Jesuits. It is situated in the river valley of the same name. Afterwards the river turns northwest, flowing on the west side of San Antonio pass, whose mountains run from north to south.

After crossing the narrow valley one enters the cañada of San Antonio. After traveling four leagues through it and climbing several small hills, we camped at the foot of the San Antonio pass, near a small stream in a ravine, usually dry. In every direction were a number of nameless sierras. Chigaguilla range was to the north.

To the Mission Guebabi.

On the 19th we traveled ten leagues northwest. Going by way of the short San Antonio pass, following along a very easy valley without any major interruptions for five leagues, we came out into the San Luis or Buenavista valley. The Santa María de Suamca river flows through this valley and we crossed it again. On its southern banks are the ranchos of Santa Bárbara, San Francisco, San Luis and Buenavista, all deserted because of Apache hostility. Their *gente de razón* owners have taken refuge at Terrenate and Tubac where they are perishing. From the entrance to this valley the road runs alongside the river five leagues from its crossing to the Guebabi mission. The mission is inhabited by fifty Pimas Altos Indians, formerly administered by Jesuits.

To the Presidio of San Ignacio de Tubac.

On the 20th we traveled eight leagues toward the northwest slightly north through the valley of the preceding day and always skirting the river. It is well-wooded by cottonwoods on its banks and the rest of the plain has many mesquites and other trees. The surrounding hills are quite bare. Among them, on the right, can be seen the Santa Rita range with its very high peak, and that of San Cayetano, remarkable as a refuge for the enemy after their forays. Two leagues from Guebabi is the small pueblo of Calabazas formerly of the Pimas Altos who perished in a bad epidemic. It was repopulated by Pápagos. Five miles from this place is the Tumacácori pueblo of the same nation, both dependent on the Guebabi mission, the latter being one league from the presidio of San Ignacio de Tubac. Tubac is situated, according to my observations, in 32°3′ north latitude and in 252°24′ longitude, by the Tenerife meridian.

The map I drew reveals the size and surroundings of this presidio, which was established on the same footing as the two preceding in 1752, during the time of the Most Excellent Señor Viceroy, Count of Revilla Gigedo. In each one of them his Majesty has fifty guns, fifty lances, and as many swords, and forty leather jackets with which to arm the civilians whenever it is necessary. There are also in each of them four four-pounder cannon cast in Mexico, neither good looking nor well made. Two of these at Tubac are totally useless because fire flashes from cracks in the breech. The majority of the others are rusty and that, plus the ignorance of the people handling them, has caused many accidents.

JANUARY, 1767

To La Ciénega.

We remained here reviewing the presidio until the fifth of this month. On that date we set out for the Altar presidio, traveling ten leagues, the first two and a half toward the west slightly southwest until we came to the summit of the Aribaca pass. Just before this we came upon a mediocre placer mine. In this distance there are several very long and steep slopes. From the pass to La Ciénega there are six leagues of rolling rocky hills leading to the southwest. The road improves in the last league and passes through a cañada surrounded on all sides by low hills covered with coarse grass as far as Longoreña, a league and a half beyond La Ciénega. We camped there néar a fresh water creek about a gunshot away. La Ciénega silver mine is at present abandoned. Neither is work being done in the little camp of El Aribaca, which lies a league to the right of the road and another league from La Ciénega, from where its ruins can be seen.

About ten leagues north of La Longoreña the high sierra of Babuquiri can be seen. This marks the end of his Majesty's dominions in this part and is the border of the Papaguería, where many gold mines are said to exist.

To the Mission of Sariqui.

On the sixth we traveled eight leagues south-southwest, the first two by a narrow canyon that serves as a bed for the creek which flows to Longoreña and ends in a short but very steep pass. Then we came to Las Tres Bellotas valley. It was much more open and unobstructed, although there were oak groves as on the preceding day. After traveling six leagues we came to another valley toward the west-northwest. We camped a quarter of a league from the entrance near a spring.

On the 7th we traveled eight leagues south-southwest, the first five through the valley of the preceding day, which we followed from the time we left our camp until we reached El Busani, pueblo *de visita* of the mission of Sariqui. The mission was recently depopulated by an epidemic, leaving only four families who were transferred to this settlement. One league before this one sees, to the left, the Arizona hill where those famous pure silver nuggets were found. Most of them weighed 160 *arrobas*. There is a spring on the left of the road about a quarter of a league from Busani. It gives rise to a creek which runs through Sariqui. These two pueblos are three leagues apart, with the Busani pass half-way between. One begins the ascent to this pass after emerging from a valley three quarters of

a league long. There is another quarter of a league to the
summit, where, taking a southeasterly course, one descends
over several hills to the said mission at the foot of the last
hill and on the banks of the creek which I have mentioned.
The banks of this creek are lined with trees. The mission is
inhabited by 300 persons, Pimas Altos administered by a
Jesuit father. This figure does not include some 200 savages of the Pápago nation who were camped in its vicinity.
These people come here in winter to escape the barrenness
and drought of their country and they return to their
homes in summertime during the rainy season. For this
reason no missions have been founded among these extremely docile Indians.

Near Las Bolas de la Arizona a small settlement was
made by civilized people at Ojo Caliente. It was abandoned
last year on account of the constant attacks of the Apaches.

Among the people of the Sariqui settlement there are
sixty armed men. In the pueblo *de visita* called Aquimuri,
two leagues to the east, thirty men can be armed from the
fifteen families there. They are also Pimas Altos or Upper
Pimas, a warlike nation respected among the Indians.

To the Mission of Tubutama.

On the 8th we traveled eight leagues. The route skirted
the Busani river over very broken ground full of mesquites, huizaches, and other trees revealing the hot climate
of the area from the descent to Sariqui. The first four
leagues were through a valley which runs south and slightly
southeast. At the end of it and up a quarter of a league
there is a pass called La Estancia. After leaving this, the
road goes through a valley similar to the preceding as far
as Tubutama. From the beginning of the ascent to the pass
the road turns south-southwest. This mission has the same
number of people as the preceding one and they are administered by a Jesuit. During this day's journey one sees only

high sierras and hills in every direction, as are found everywhere after leaving Tubac.

To the Presidio of Santa Gertrudis del Altar.

On the 9th we traveled 12 leagues to the southwest over level land and skirting the same river. There were continuous woods of fairly high mesquites, huizaches, cat's claws, gourds, greenwood trees, órganos, zaguares, pitahayas, etc., and very little pasture, on account of the saltpeter in the earth. Two leagues farther on is Santa Teresa, the pueblo *de visita* of Tubutama, with an equal number of people of the same nation. In its neighborhood there was a Pápago village with grass huts like those in the pueblos. Three leagues farther on is the pueblo of Ati, and four from this the mission of Oquilva, both of the same nation and having the same population. Three leagues farther on is the presidio of Santa Gertrudis del Altar, situated, according to my observations, in 31°2′ north latitude and in 250°39′ longitude, by the Tenerife meridian. In it there is a company on the same footing as the other companies of Sonora, but not established for the same purpose. This one is designed to restrain the Seris, rebellious Pimas, and Pápagos should they at any time attempt to unite, as happened in the uprising of 1752. Besides the soldiers there are twenty-five families and ten armed men, for which his Majesty has a supply of arms just as in other presidios. The situation and arrangement of this presidio is shown on the map. The distance to the coast of the Gulf of California is thirty-two leagues west passing by Pitiqui six leagues farther on. The settlement has forty families. Two leagues and a half from this is Caborca with sixty families administered by a Jesuit missionary. Six leagues farther on in the same direction is the Bisani pueblo, composed of thirty-six families, all Pimas Altos. This, as well as Pitiqui, is a pueblo *de visita* of the said mission.

To Rancho Santa Ana.

On the 23rd of the same month, after the review, we set out for the town and presidio of San Miguel de Horcasitas. We traveled ten leagues east over level ground covered with continuous woods of mesquites, huizaches, and other trees characteristic of a hot climate. On our right was the high sierra of Carnero and on the left the Oquitoa. After traveling through a small pass one comes to the abandoned rancho of Ocuca on the slope. We camped in a valley not far from a lagoon. A great many unbranded cattle and strays are gathered between here and Pitic. This area abounds in good pasture.

On the 24th we traveled eight long leagues in the same direction and over identical terrain as the day before. We slept at Santa Ana, a rancho of Spaniards who are almost ruined by constant attacks and robberies of the rebellious Seris and Pimas Altos.

To Santa Magdalena.

On the 25th we traveled eight leagues to the northeast skirting from the start the small San Ignacio river, which rises in the valley of the same name. This valley is from a quarter to half a league wide and is formed by two mountain ranges, those on the right being very high, and named Los Remedios and Dolores; those to the left have no special name. In the first league there is an abundant spring and near it are the ruins of the Santa Marta rancho. Three leagues farther on are the burned houses of the small San Lorenzo pueblo. Most of the civilized inhabitants perished in the fires set by the Seris ten years ago. Two leagues farther up is Santa Magdalena, inhabited by thirty-six families of Pimas Altos. It is the pueblo *de visita* of the mission San Ignacio two leagues away. We slept there that night. In it are 300 persons of the same nation and sixty braves as soldiers. They were administered by a Jesuit who was also in charge of the Imoris pueblo situated to the north at the confluence of another river, which empties into the San Ignacio.

To the Pueblo and Mission of Cucurpe.

On the 26th we traveled seven leagues south over low hills covered with pasture and mesquites. After traversing six leagues we saw, on our right, the abandoned Sásabe rancho where there are some wild cattle. One league from this is Los Alamos. We camped there at the foot of the Cordillera de la Soledad, with the Cucurpe pass to the south.

On the 27th we traveled eight leagues principally south-southeast. The first two and three quarters leagues ran through a valley to the foot of the Cucurpe pass. The ascent is a quarter of a league long and very steep. From the summit we came down for about a league over several hills to the Cucurpe valley where there is a small perennial spring. After traveling through this valley four leagues over an occasional small hill and through thick woods for the entire day, we forded a small river whose source is in the sierra of Los Dolores. At this place, where the river is augmented by that of the Saracache, there are mines and gold placers. Very few people work there for fear of the Apaches who have almost destroyed it. They attack travelers daily in this pass and its vicinity, approaching it sheltered by the Sierra Madre and the thickets and gullies. After we crossed the river we came to the Cucurpe pueblo situated on a hill. It is an Opata mission cared for by Jesuits.

On the other side of the sierra that forms the Cucurpe pass there is another pass by which one goes to the Cocospera and Santa María Suamca valleys. There is also another valley up the San Ignacio river with several settlements, which, with very little effort, could be protected by the presidio of Terrenate.

To the Mission of Opodepe and Pueblo Nacameri.

On the 28th we traveled thirteen leagues southeast by east through a canyon between two very high mountain ranges that were almost interlocking. The enormous precipices of the two ranges form a gorge through which the San Miguel river flows. We crossed it seventy-three times during the day's journey. In three leagues one comes to the San Xavier smelter on a small plain or plaza. It has been depopulated by the constant hostilities of the Seris. Two ore crushers and a smelting furnace still exist and, although it is risky, some of the settlers occasionally use them. They bring loads of ore from the mine four or five leagues away, which they make into small silver bars, extracting four marks [32 ounces] to the load. Three leagues away is the little Indian pueblo called Tuape, dependent upon the Cucurpe mission, and of the same nation. Almost everybody there was infected by a violent epidemic of *tabardillos*. From here to Opodepe is seven leagues. The road extends along a river bed through country more open and less rocky, but covered with woods and in places impenetrable. In this valley there are a number of ranchos which have been depopulated by the Seris who are constantly in these parts. For this reason passage through this canyon is infinitely dangerous. The enemy, taking advantage of the heights, can easily kill all those who are below them in the canyon, where they can neither defend themselves nor turn back. Finally, in much more open country with only hills surrounding it, near the left side of the road on a hill, there is a small settlement of civilized people called El Realito. It precedes by a league the Opodepe mission where we spent the night. The Indians who live in it are Opatas and were administered by a Jesuit.

On the 29th we traveled eight leagues in the same direction through the valley of the previous day, equally wooded, but with fewer sierras. Following the course of the river which we forded four or five times, we halted at Nacameri, pueblo *de visita* of Opodepe, inhabited by Indians of the same nation and some civilized people.

To San Miguel de Horcasitas.

On the 30th we traveled nine leagues in the same direction over a very bad road until we came out of the canyon. One league farther the San Miguel river is crossed again, and over a number of rocky hills one comes to the canyon two leagues away. It extends two more leagues over ground covered with boulders where horses can scarcely get a foothold. This area is more dangerous than any part of Sonora. Upon leaving it one comes to La Tinaja a league away, and in another league the ruined pueblo of Populo is reached. It was inhabited by the Seris. One league beyond is the town of San Miguel de Horcasitas, situated, according to my observations in 29°44′ north latitude and 253°23′ longitude, by the Tenerife meridian.

On the map that I drew, its shape and arrangement are shown, as well as that of the presidio which is garrisoned by a cavalry company, with the same number of soldiers and the same allowance as the other presidios. The captain is the governor and has his residence here because it is the capital of the Province of Sonora. There are also sixty civilians and various Indian families who are the servants. All are very poor.

FEBRUARY

To the Mission of Los Ures.

The review of this presidio detained us until the 23rd of this month. Then we set out for Buenavista presidio, traveling twelve leagues east-southeast, nine of them through a valley thickly wooded with shrubs typical of hot country. We went as far as a small pass, preceded by a stone corral, where the Apaches often travel. After that we continued over low wooded hills to Los Ures mission. A quarter of a league before reaching it we forded the Sonora river which passes through the pueblo. The mission, inhabited by as many as 200 families of Opatas and Pimas and thirty civilized people, is administered by a Jesuit. It is situated in the pleasant Sonora valley on the banks of the river, where the inhabitants collect all kinds of seeds. In its architecture and church ornaments it excels all the other missions. We did not travel on the 24th.

To Santa Rosalía.

On the 25th we went twelve leagues south on level ground covered by mesquite, etc. After eight leagues we came to Casita hill. On the right the San Cosme and San Damián hills stand out as landmarks. They are very similar and greatly elevated above the chain which unites them. From there it is seven leagues to Santa Rosalía, the pueblo of San Joseph de Gracia, and the Real de Minas del Gavilán. All of them are abandoned because of the attacks of the Seris, who have their assemblies in the vicinity. These places are seldom visited by the Apaches who are not usually in the vicinity of Ures. On the left, at an equal distance, the Cerro de Quisuani stands out. In this stretch, abounding in pasture but without water, live an infinite number of stray and wild cattle. These animals drink in the arroyo at the foot of Santa Rosalía, where we halted, and in other distant waterholes. There is no other water on the whole road except the Agua Bendita spring in a little ravine at a short distance from our point of departure. Thirty families of Pimas Altos compose the population of

Santa Rosalía which is the pueblo *de visita* of the Ures mission. To prevent its destruction a detachment of thirty men and one officer are kept there. These men are drawn from all the presidios near Cerro Prieto under whose protection it is maintained.

To San Joseph de los Pimas.

On the 26th we traveled nine leagues southeast one quarter south over ground like that of the preceding day. We camped in a deserted spot with nothing of particular interest but a small hill made of rocks piled on top of one another. They had such a resonance that when struck purposely by stones thrown by some boys, a sound resembling a chime was produced and we could hear it half a league from the mission and another half from the hill. The tones were finer than the peals of ordinary bells and somewhat resembled the sound produced by bells made with silver alloy, which was even more unusual as these rocks have no metal in them whatever, as has been proved by repeated experiments with fire and quicksilver.

On the 27th we traveled eight leagues southeast one quarter south through country similar to that of the preceding day. Four leagues before arriving at San Joseph de Pimas an opening between the sierra Del Chivato and some rolling hills can be seen to the southwest. From there a part of Cerro Prieto can be seen some fifteen leagues away. This runs from north to south and is some forty-five to fifty leagues in circumference, according to experts. On the left the plain ends in the Quisuani and Cobaichi hills. Near them runs another road where there is water for human consumption. We halted at San Joseph de los Pimas, where there are sixty-four Indian families of that nation. A company of militia cavalrymen was kept there to prevent attacks by the Seris.

To Tecoripa Mission.

On the 28th we traveled fifteen leagues east, although the road makes a turn forming a semicircle in a southerly direction, over level land covered with mesquite, huizaches, and palo verde. From this area they obtain tar, fern, some barilla, hard wood, and Brazil wood. At three leagues there is a small canyon called Las Bolas and after three more we came to the Laguna Pedregosa, which we found dry. Midway along the road is the place called La Cruz, where the Salvia plain begins and there is a great abundance of sage. Later one comes to the Agua Caliente and, after continuing for a half league along the bed of the arroyo formed by it, arrives at the Tecoripa mission where there are twenty-five Pima families. Here we halted.

The most notable mountains seen from the road are those of Los Pilares to the southwest stretching approximately from north to south and ending at Yaqui. In this direction there is also the abandoned rancho of San Lorenzo at the foot of a mountain which has a needle-like pinnacle. Near by is a swamp and along its grassy edges a great number of wild cattle graze. To the northeast are the Comari mountains and other nameless peaks enclosing the plain on all sides.

MARCH

To Comuripa Mission.

On the first we traveled nine leagues south-southeast over rolling hills with the same woods as on preceding days. The first league we traveled along the bed of the same arroyo which goes through the pueblo. Two leagues before reaching Suaqui we were again following the creek and we forded it several times in that distance. In the intervening road there are several ravines to be crossed, among them that of Uvas Lamas. We halted at the village of

Suaqui composed of thirty families of Lower Pimas. Like those of the preceding village, the inhabitants of this pueblo have been considerably diminished since the uprising of January, 1766.

On the 2nd we traveled ten leagues in the same direction over land like the preceding. The first two and a half leagues were traveled along the bed of the Suaqui creek. The Cosari empties into it a short distance from the pueblo. Two leagues before arriving at the Comuripa mission of Lower Pimas which is in charge of a Jesuit, one fords the said creek. Its banks are covered with carrizal grass. Several mountains are visible in the distance. Among them to the west is the Bacatete, and the continuation of the Cordillera of Los Pilares, the usual Seri refuge.

In all the hills and arroyos of these last two days' journey to the Comuripa mission there is gold-bearing gravel and sand which is not mined because of the obvious danger of being butchered by the enemies.

To the Presidio of Buenavista.

On the 3rd we traveled twelve leagues southeast through the Comuripa valley. The Yaqui river flows through the valley a short distance from this mission. The creek which passes by the mission empties into the river. Skirting the Yaqui river for seven leagues one comes to the little Tubac pass. Its name is also given to the adjacent valley. It is thickly wooded like the one preceding as far as Buenavista presidio. This presidio is situated on a hill on the right bank of the said river in 28° north latitude and 257° longitude by the Tenerife meridian. At this presidio, besides the company which is equal to the others in Sonora in the number of soldiers and their allowance, there are sixty families of Lower Pimas, which make up the Comuripa pueblo *de visita*.

To Hacienda de San Salvador de los Cedros.

On the 16th, after the review, we set out from this presidio and traveled twelve leagues. At the foot of the hill
we forded the Yaqui river. Then the road continues south-
southeast for ten leagues over a thickly wooded plain to the
very high and long Santa Ana pass. Two leagues preceding it is the abandoned rancho of Mochomobampo. Two
leagues after leaving that pass one comes to the Mutica
rancho, also deserted. We camped there. The direction of
this last stretch of road is toward the east-northeast along
the edge of a small stream which flows down through a
narrow valley formed by two very high mountain chains.
All the country in this day's journey is under the jurisdiction of the province of Ostimuri, which begins on the left
bank of the river.

On the 17th we traveled six leagues to the east-northeast
over level ground, less broken than that of the previous
day. We slept at the hacienda of San Salvador de los
Cedros, otherwise called Tesopaco. It is inhabited by several Spanish families, augmented by those who were living
at the ranchos of La Lima, La Pirinola, etc. which were
abandoned because of constant Seri attacks. The only
noteworthy things near the road are the Pirinola hill a
short distance to the left, and the mining town of Baroyeca
nine leagues to the right of Tesopaco. There are still
droves of mares, notwithstanding that the enemies have
driven off a great many. We did not travel on the 18th.

To the Mining Town of Trinidad de Arriba.

On the 19th we traveled ten leagues, the first four northeast over a wooded plain. On leaving the hacienda one
crosses a small stream in this plain. At the end of it is the
Santa Rosa pass, one league long, with a very troublesome
stony ascent. It lies to the northeast and the descent from
the winding summit is between north and west and leads

to a narrow valley through which an arroyo runs. The footing is the same as the preceding day. At the end of a league to the north there is a narrow canyon from which one emerges into a valley. To the right of the entrance there are remains of the Nuri garden land which was depopulated when the Seris killed the inhabitants. Four leagues to the northwest is the Nuri pueblo composed of thirty families of Yaquis and Mayos and subject to the Jesuit missionary at Mobas, three leagues to the northwest.

On the 20th we traveled nine leagues north, slightly northeast over rough thickly wooded hills. Among them it is necessary to cross two very high and rugged ranges. There is also an arroyo to be forded several times before reaching the deserted Curea rancho, seven leagues away, where there are some horses and cattle. We camped two leagues beyond it at an unnamed waterhole.

On the 21st we traveled eighteen leagues. In the first league to the north-northwest one descends to the narrow and very rocky Guadalupe valley. There is considerable water from Milpillas creek which runs along the San Antonio de la Huerta road toward the south. After traveling six leagues and making several turns between east and north, on a height to the left one sees La Quema rancho, burned by the Seris after they had killed all the people. Two leagues farther on is San Nicolás rancho, also depopulated. Four leagues from the latter one leaves the valley and, taking the road on the left to the northeast, one begins the climb to the San Antonio ridge, one of the most rugged of the Sierra Madre in this area. There are a number of steep rocky declivities in it, especially from the mining camp of Enmedio to Arriba camp. The distance from the foot of the ridge to the top is one league, followed by ups and downs for another two leagues to the mining camp of Abajo. At that place there are only a few people; the same is true of Enmedio. One league from the latter is the mining town of Trinidad de Arriba where a part of the people from the other two have gone because of the failure of their mines. They are supported by working the two remaining mines, which yield as much as twenty ounces to the load. Because of the lack of money and men, however, very little ore is taken out. There are eighty families in this settlement, several of them Europeans, governed by an alcalde mayor and administered by a parish priest.

On the 22nd and 23rd we did not travel.

To Yécora.

On the 24th we traveled eight leagues east. We spent the night at Yécora which is inhabited by forty-five families of Pimas, a pueblo of the Onapa mission, both in charge of a Jesuit.

On leaving Trinidad one ascends a very rugged steep ridge, immediately followed by that of El Balcón, which is much higher. The road descending from the summit is much smoother, although there are several hills before reaching the little Marcelo rancho, six and a half leagues away from the mining camp. From there the road runs through a gentle valley with a creek flowing east. After passing a small canyon it extends to the Yécora pueblo, a league and a half from the said rancho. To the north of the latter the creek flows near by. On the entire road there are many extraordinarily tall pine trees and a great deal of red grass, which is the only pasture in this whole Sierra Madre after leaving Nuri where the rugged area begins.

To Arroyo Hondo.

On the 25th we traveled ten leagues east over several crests less high and rugged than those of the preceding day. Among them are some stretches of reasonably good road through several small valleys. The first is four leagues from Yécora and is called La Cevadilla. It has a

small creek. Four leagues beyond are the Pilares. These
are perpendicular cuts in a piece of sierra forming a
deep gorge and having a stream running through it. One
league from Los Pilares is Los Mulatos river running
from south to north in this area. It can be forded in shallow water. This river flows into the Río Grande or Yaqui.
Another league farther on is the abandoned site of San
Miguel where we camped in some fields near a small
stream.

On the 26th we traveled nine leagues, the first two to
the east. Afterwards we turned northeast through a canyon until we reached Maicoba. It is inhabited by forty
families of Pima Indians, and is a pueblo *de visita* of the
Mori mission. The mission is situated fourteen leagues to
the south and has a hot climate because the road descends
for this whole distance. Both places are in charge of a
Jesuit. From Maicoba to Arroyo Hondo lay six leagues of
hills and some less troublesome valleys. The first one is
two leagues long beginning at the point of departure from
the pueblo and going northeast as we did for the rest of
the road. Very high mountains covered with pines and
madrones in the immense ravines are visible in the vicinity.
The jurisdiction of Sonora terminates at Arroyo Hondo
and that of Nueva Vizcaya begins.

DESCRIPTION OF THE PROVINCE OF SONORA

The government of the province of Sonora includes within its jurisdiction Ostimuri and Sinaloa whose location is indicated on the general map. I shall confine myself to the description of the first, since it is the actual theater of the war with the rebellious Seris and Pimas. Living in its center, they are gradually destroying it like thieves in the house. Together with the Gileño Apaches, who attack it from the north, they are penetrating farther and farther every day, and have now reached the neighborhood of San Miguel de Horcasitas.

This very rich and fertile province is situated between 28° and 33° north latitude and between 250° and 258° longitude, reckoning by the Pico de Theide meridian on the island of Santa Cruz de Tenerife. It is bounded on the west and north by the savage Pápagos and Pimas Altos who live on the Gila river, and the Gileño Apaches; on the east and south by the provinces of Nueva Vizcaya with the Sierra Madre serving as a dividing line; in those places named, by the Ostimuri mountains and the Gulf of California, now in the possession of the Seris and the rebellious Pimas from Guaymas to Caborca.

It is subdivided into the following districts: Villa de San Miguel de Horcasitas, where the governor resides; Matape and Quisuani; Nuestra Señora de Guadalupe de la Ventana; Santa Ana de Tepache valley; Oposura; the mining town of Nacozari; Corodeguachi or Fronteras; the mining town of Motepore; La Concepción; the mining town of Soyopa; Opodepe valley; and Pimería Alta. These locations, together with the pueblos which they contain, will be indicated on the general map. These settlements are composed of some Spaniards and the following Indians — Opatas, Pimas Altos and Pimas Bajos, Tobas, Egues, Tubaris or Eudebes, Yaquis, Mayos, Toros, Chois, and Guaymas, all governed by alcaldes mayores or Spanish lieutenants appointed by the governor. In each Indian pueblo there are also *magistrates* named from among themselves, but in general the pueblos were administered by Jesuits. At San Miguel and other mining camps, in which the citizens are Spaniards, mestizos, and mulattoes, there are clerical curates, subject to the bishopric of Durango, to which this province belongs in spiritual matters. In temporal it belongs to the Audiencia de Guadalajara. The swamps and hills nearby are also inhabited by the Salineros, Carrizos, and Tepocas, known by the name of Seris. They are destroying this province, attacking whenever they please because they live in the center of it. And, since they know the country perfectly, they are able to find a thousand places of refuge in the rough crags of its mountains.

The climate is extreme. In their respective seasons cold and heat are severe. It is more inclined, however, to be a hot country, especially the valleys of the mountainous regions where it is necessary to live and plant crops because of the scarcity of water in the plains and on the heights. All kinds of seeds are gathered there, because the land yields abundant crops with very little labor. Pasture is excellent and abundant. Consequently many mules, horses, and cattle of all kinds used to breed there, but they have been exterminated by constant raids of Seris and Apaches. There are immense woods of mesquites, huizaches, cat's claw, and other shrubbery of the hot country, which combined with órganos, pitahayas, zaguaros, zaramullos, and other exotic plants make the woods impenetrable in some places. Cottonwood, ash, and alder trees grow profusely on the banks of creeks where some fish are caught. In the higher regions many pines and oaks are found, and the thickets shelter an infinite number of brown bears, coyotes, wolves, wild cats, and much game of all kinds. There are more than enough venomous animals, such as rattlesnakes and *dragones* which are the most important. In compensation for these annoyances and the unhealthiness of the country that is subject to fevers, especially in Pimería Alta where the water is bad, providence has shown part of its power in the gold, silver, and pearls with which it has enriched the country. Virgin metals crop out everywhere in the hills and valleys.

This province is being attacked, as I have already said, by the Seri Indians and the Gileño Apaches whose customary hideouts and entries I am going to explain, beginning with the Apaches.

The Sierra Madre lies between the presidio of Janos in Nueva Vizcaya and the presidio of Fronteras in Sonora. The Gileños have a free passage through these mountains by the Carretas ridge, which they frequent, and over the Caguiona mountains; by El Potrero in the Fronteras chain and by other passages named in the diary. From the shelter of these immense and rugged mountains they sally forth to attack all the neighboring valleys and settlements belonging to the two districts.

Between Fronteras and the presidio of Terrenate, the most prominent mountains where the enemies usually seek refuge are Mababe or Tesocomáchic, Magallanes, Chiguicagui, where there are always many Apaches villages, and Agua Verde.

From Terrenate to Tubac presidio their sallies are over Las Bolas ridge, the San Antonio pass, and San Luis valley. In the neighborhood of the presidio are the San Cayetano and Santa Rita mountains. In the last named is the Consumidero pass, ten leagues northeast of the presidio and much used by the enemies. These mountains continue as a chain four or five leagues beyond Tucson pueblo,

located twenty-one leagues north of Tubac and five from
San Xavier del Bac which precedes it. Both are inhabited
by Pimas Altos Indians and administered by a Jesuit missionary. They are the most advanced outposts on the
whole frontier. Consequently a small detachment of soldiers and a corporal from the Tubac company are maintained in them. With this very small force they defend
themselves admirably against the Gila Apaches, whom
they punish occasionally because they are the most warlike.
The distance from Tucson to the Gila river, traveling
north, is approximately fifty leagues. On its banks are the
ruins of an ancient town known by the name of Casas
Grandes. It is said to have originated from the earliest
Indian nations who came from the north to establish themselves in these areas.

From Tubac presidio looking toward Altar one sees the
ruins of the Real del Aribaca, the Longoreña mine, and
the Real de la Arizona. The first two were abandoned
during the uprising of the Upper Pimas in the year '52.
The Indians were subdued after defeat by our forces on the
slopes of the Cerro de Bubuquiburi. On that occasion they
suffered great destruction without any loss on our part, notwithstanding the fact that they greatly outnumbered us.
Longoreña mine was abandoned because of the constant
attacks of the Apaches who frequent the cordillera where
it was situated, and because of the proclamation that no
individual could work in this camp except under his
Majesty's auspices.

The Altar presidio is free from Apache attacks, but not
from those of the Seris and rebellious Pimas. These two
advance in this vicinity by way of the Sierra del Oro, the
Carrizal de Picú, El Tecolote, and the Cornelio slopes,
from which they infest Soledad, Santa Ana, the pueblos of
Caborca, Pitiqui, and Bisani. The regions usually inhabited by the enemies are as follows: Totayuca, thirty-five

leagues southwest of Altar; Aribaipía, five leagues south; Los Pozos de la Trinidad, otherwise known as Mezcal sierra, sixty leagues south on the coast; the Espuelas ranges; Cajón de la Higuera; and El Bausa, three or four leagues apart from each other and thirty-six from the presidio to the south. The enemies also occupy the rest of the coast, named the marshes, as far as Guaymas pass or Yaqui river. Their principal hiding place is the Island of Tiburón on which there are fourteen small waterholes. On the opposite coast of Sonora, which is called the Upanguaymas swamps, there is a spring sufficient for 300 horses in the driest season, although there is no pasture within twelve leagues. Half a league north, on the other side of a small ridge which extends to the sea, is the place where the enemies embark for that island. From there, as well as from neighboring marshes, they enter Santa Ana and the Opodepe valley via the Cornelio slopes, the Bacuache ridge and canyon from which they fall upon Cucurpe, by way of Sierra Dolores and the Cajón de Policarpio to the Bacuache range. They continue to make a frontier of the marshes of the Carnero mountains twenty-five leagues from San Miguel. The great majority of the enemy resides at Tecolote, Aguas Frías, Carrizal, Las Pilas de Ybarburu, Agua Amarilla, Siete Cerritos, Tenuaya, El Pitic, Cerro Prieto, and the Sierra de Pilares terminating in the Yaqui river, an area extending from twenty to twenty-five leagues. Because of the thickets in this region and the ruggedness of the canyons by which they actually enter, they believe themselves to be secure. All of this country suffers a scarcity of water in dry season. The total numbers of Seris, Pimas Altos, and Pimas Bajos is estimated to be four hundred fighting men.

JURISDICTION OF NUEVA VIZCAYA

To the Pueblo and Mission of Tomóchic.

On the 27th, continuing our route, we traveled seven leagues, principally northeast. We climbed over a great deal of very uncomfortable footing and loose rocks, especially in the creek beds we passed before reaching Yepachi, pueblo *de visita* of Tutuaca mission. One hundred Pimas Altos families live here under the jurisdiction of Nueva Vizcaya.

On the 28th we traveled eight leagues principally east-northeast over a road somewhat less troublesome and less rocky than the previous day, although there are several rocky ridges to be climbed. On the high mountains in the vicinity there are many liveoaks, common oaks, and other trees native to cold country, for it is very cold here because it is the highest elevation and in the center of the mountains. Going on for a short distance through a canyon where a small stream flows down into the Río Grande, after passing several other creeks we arrived at Tutuaca, the first pueblo of Tarahumara Alta, with its seventy families administered by a Jesuit.

We spent the 29th at this pueblo, and in the night of the 28th-29th a light snow fell.

On the 30th we traveled nine leagues to the east. We found several ridges, among them La Banderilla, which is very steep and high. The rest of the road goes through a valley along the banks of a creek which flowed in the direction we were heading. Coming out of it through a small canyon, we entered that of La Virgen and camped at the end of it.

On the 31st we traveled five leagues east. The road was better and with fewer ridges than that of the preceding day. Several times we skirted and forded the same arroyo which runs through a valley. It has bad stretches. At the end of it is Tomóchic, pueblo and mission of Tarahumares where a hundred families are administered by a Jesuit. Also under his care were the pueblos of Arescachic with ninety families, Pagueachic with forty, and Tajulichic with one hundred families, all of the same nation.

APRIL

To the Mining Town of Cosaguarichi.

On the 1st we traveled eight leagues east over several ridges with many loose rocks. At seven leagues one comes to the Tesorachi valley. We traveled through the valley about one league over tillable land to the Agua Caliente valley. After passing through another small valley with a small stream, we came to Tesorachi, pueblo and mission of Tarahumares, administered by a Jesuit. North of it is Arescachic.

On the 2nd we traveled ten leagues southeast, the first five over a range having several creeks, followed by a sharp very rocky ascent which precedes the Tonachi plain. We traveled five leagues to Pichera, pueblo *de visita* of Temaichic, three leagues to the south. Both are inhabited by Tarahumares, the number of whose families in the first is approximately twenty. This plain extends from south to north for ten to twelve leagues and the road runs in this direction to the valley, which lay to our left.

On the 3rd we traveled nine leagues, the first five over rocky ridges. A stretch of sloping valley precedes a plain where the old rancho of Temaichic is situated. From this, one takes a road to the left leading to the new rancho of the same name. On the top of a small hill nearby is another parting of roads, one going to Temaichic, and the one which we followed to the Guillermo rancho, four leagues to the east. There we halted.

On the 4th we traveled eight leagues, the first six toward the east. The plain of the previous day terminates at a large, deep lagoon, commonly called La Lagunita. It lies a short distance to the left of the road and it has water all year. This is not the case with two other smaller lagoons on the right which we passed a little earlier. Usually they dry up. From here one takes the road to the southeast through some extensive hills and afterwards through a valley. Two leagues from the lagoon is the mining town of Cosaguarichi. It is in ruins and inhabited by about a hundred families of Spaniards, mestizos, and mulattoes, with some Indian laborers who work in the mines. Although Servando is the best mine and a rich one, it is worked very little because of the incapacity of its owner. These people are governed by an alcalde mayor and administered in spiritual matters by a parish priest who also has in his charge the small unimportant mining camp of Poliachi and some small ranchos.

This mining camp and its neighborhood are severely harassed by enemy Apaches. They come from the foot hills and slopes of the Sierra Madre, taking refuge in it when it suits them, especially in nearby Cerro Prieto. They rarely penetrate the range and for this reason the pueblos of Tarahumara Alta, situated in the interior and most rugged part of the Sierra Madre, are seldom troubled by them.

To the Pueblo of Bobonoyaba.

On the 5th we did not travel. On the 6th we traveled twelve leagues, the first five to the east through the valley where the camp is situated. From there one takes the road southeast passing over a very steep ridge and a stretch of valley terminating in a rise and finally comes to a mesa covered with much pasture and some liveoaks. This mesa is six leagues long. From it one descends to a little valley where Copete creek flows. We found it dry. Skirting it for one league, we came to several charcoal makers' huts scattered along its banks. We slept at the last one.

On the 7th we traveled eight leagues south-southeast over very steep rocky hills. At the end of four leagues we arrived at the little town of Santa Rosalía where thirty Tepehuanes families are administered by a clerical curate from San Lorenzo. Dependent upon it also is Las Cuevas pueblo composed of an equal number of Tepehuanes families. We stopped there to sleep.

On the 8th we traveled nine leagues over ground like the preceding. At the end of the first four leagues which are traveled south one quarter southeast, the San Pedro river is forded in shallow water. On its banks are several charcoal makers' huts. Five leagues from this to the southeast is San Xavier rancho, situated on the small creek of the same name. Near the very bare road, to the left a league and a half from the ford of the San Pedro river, was the Satebo pueblo. At four leagues is the Bobonoyaba pueblo subject to the curate of the former place and inhabited by some civilized people and Tepehuanes Indians.

To the Valley of San Bartolomé.

On the 9th we traveled eight leagues. At the outset we climbed a hill to reach the plain, then we traveled six leagues southeast reaching the Agua Nueva pass. Turning again to the east, one goes through a valley a quarter of a league wide, preceded by some bare hills. Two leagues farther is Los Belduques rancho on the bank of an arroyo which proceeds from a spring in the Agua Nueva pass. Many sheep, cows, and horses are raised there. Two leagues beyond this place to the west, upstream, is the Santa Cruz de Valerio hacienda.

On the 10th we traveled eight leagues, the first to the east through a valley in which the aforesaid hacienda is situated, to the place called La Boca where the valley ends. Immediately on entering the Chihuahua highway we traveled seven leagues south-southeast over level land with an occasional small hill and much loose rock to the hacienda of Nuestra Señora del Pilar. This hacienda is situated on the left bank of the Conchos river which flows northeast and passes the abolished presidio of the same name some thirty leagues farther on.

Along the road are several small ranchos on Belduques creek. Half-way we came to the hacienda La Jabonera. In the neighborhood a number of sierras were visible and in the space they embraced was some pasture and mesquite.

On the 11th we traveled nine leagues, five of them to the southeast over a low rocky range to a small pass whose ascent is southeast one quarter east. From there the road is somewhat better. It follows the same route as far as the Sapiain hacienda on the other side of a small creek. No more water is found on this day's journey except some small pools at the foot of the pass mentioned. The surrounding country has little pasture.

On the 12th we traveled ten leagues southeast over gentle hills. At six leagues we came to San Gregorio hacienda on the right bank of a small stream which runs through a cultivated valley. There are also two springs whose waters, retained by two dams, are used to run a mill and irrigate the land thus obviating need of river water. From here to the San Bartolomé valley is four leagues. In all the area covered in today's and yesterday's journey there is plenty of pasture and some horses and mules are raised. Mountains are seen in every direction, the most important being Almoloya.

MAY

To the Presidios of Cerro Gordo and El Pasaje.

On the 5th we set out from San Bartolomé valley to review a cavalry company temporarily stationed at Cerro Gordo. We arrived on the 6th after having traveled twenty-five leagues through the same place as on our entry. This company is composed of forty-one men, including three officers and a sergeant, their annual allowance amounting to 16,665 pesos.

During the sojourn at this presidio I took the opportunity to make an observation and I find it to be situated in 26°35′ north latitude and 262°30′ longitude, reckoning by the Tenerife meridian.

On the 17th we set out from this presidio, returning to El Pasaje by the same road over which we had entered the country. We traveled the entire distance of fifty-one leagues in three days arriving on the 19th. It was necessary for us to remain until the 27th.

To Nueva Bilbao.

On the 27th we traveled three leagues principally west and mostly over rocky hills covered with mesquites, huizaches, etc. A league before reaching Cuencamé, in a chain of hills, there is a small pass with some bad stretches for vehicles. Flat-topped mesas where there are gold and silver mines stand out among the hills. A certain amount of both ores is taken out at the same Cuencamé camp, but it is worked slowly because of the incapacity of the miners.

On the 28th we did not travel. On the 29th we traveled twelve leagues, the first eight northeast over level road. Hills and mountains were visible in every direction. Afterwards one follows a canyon extending four leagues toward the east until one emerges at the foot of a very high and precipitous mountain. On our left on the way to Parras lake there was a sort of plain encircled by high mountains.

The Guanaval river runs through this area. We camped on its banks near a hut where the family of a herder was living.

To the right there is another somewhat shorter horse trail which divides near the canyon. Passing through it one finds another canyon opening to the east. The road continues north until it comes out on a plain. Noteworthy on this day's journey are the small Otate pass four leagues from the start, the Salazar pools which we found dry, and the Ledesma plain. Then follow the canyons of which I have spoken. All this country is very arid and has little grass, its products being palmillas, lechuguillas, and chamizos. Surrounding hills are also very bare.

One league north-northwest of the place where we camped is the Ximulco cattle ranch. It is located behind a high range and we reached it by going through a canyon. One league farther is the Sombreretillo cattle ranch belonging to the same owner. Although pasture is very scarce unless there are good rains in this area of irregular rainfall, the ranch was established for the purpose of raising horses and mules.

On the 30th we traveled eleven leagues mainly northeast. At the end of the plain we came to a small pass which precedes another plain also surrounded by hills, called Los Pozos de Calvo, where there is no water except when it rains. One emerges from this plain by way of Las Sorruedas canyon six leagues from the place of our departure. This canyon is five leagues long, with several small slopes, some loose rocks, and a number of little ravines which make it very troublesome. Our route varied slightly from east by north to northwest. We camped at the end of the canyon without any water, nor is there any found on this road. The products of the vicinity are the same as those of the preceding day, and the many hills which are to be seen in every direction are of the same kind.

On the 31st we traveled eight leagues, principally northeast over arid land of the same kind and with the same products as that of the preceding day. We passed the Coyotillos plain encircled by sierras. Four leagues beyond we entered San Joseph canyon which twists back and forth from north to east and even to the south for three leagues. Its greatest width is four hundred paces. This emerges upon another plain and at the end of a league is the Alamo pueblo. It is formed by a colony of Tlaxcaltecan Indians who left Parras thirty-seven years ago. Today they number 500 persons. They have several springs to irrigate their land which abounds in every kind of grain and many vines. The Indians allow a great deal of the water to be wasted and they have more than enough land. For this reason some Spanish residents have obtained permission to form a settlement under the name of La Nueva Bilbao, half a league west-southwest of the Alamo church. They had already made progress with the irrigating ditch by taking water from some copious sources called Santiago springs, one league south-southwest of the pueblo. The waters disappear entirely into a swamp. They have also begun to work on their church which they are to dedicate to Nuestra Señora de Begoña. But it is a long task for thirty poor settlers who have worked up to now without any help.

These Indians are administered by an assistant curate subject to the Parras parish and governed by a lieutenant of justice placed there by the alcalde mayor of the said town.

JUNE

To the Pueblo of Santa María de las Parras.

On the 1st we traveled six leagues northeast over level saline land surrounded by sierras covered with lechuguillas, chamizos, and mesquites, but without any pasture.

On our left was the swamp formed by the overflow of Santiago springs. We slept at the hacienda de la Peña, situated on a height at the entrance to a small pass.

On the 2nd we traveled fourteen leagues over level ground of the same nature as the preceding. Except for the first two leagues, which include the pass formed by several hills, the road is rocky. There are also some small ravines which extend northeast. One follows the same road for three more leagues to Los Charcos. Then one turns east to the San Lorenzo hacienda, commonly called Abajo. This distance is seven leagues. From here to Parras it is two short leagues. Thus it is not necessary to go by the round-about way to San Lorenzo which is two leagues longer. There are two other roads. We took the middle one because it is the best. The horse trail on the left has the advantage of water which is not found on the other two nor in their vicinity. The view toward the north reveals a chain of bare hills and to the south another similar and lofty range.

The pueblo of Santa María de las Parras owes its origin to the Tlaxcalteca nation. Later, drawn by the pleasant nature of the country, a number of Spaniards, mestizos, and mulattoes settled there. Little by little they acquired such ascendancy over the original settlers that the place can scarcely be recognized as an Indian pueblo, because of their poverty and limited number. The best part of the land is absorbed by two haciendas, San Lorenzo and one owned by the Marqués de San Miguel de Aguayo. Their principal crop consists of grapes. They make reasonably good sweet wine and very good brandy. This settlement is quite extensive. We stayed there on the third.

To the Hacienda de los Patos.

On the 4th we traveled eleven leagues principally east-northeast over level land with an occasional small hill up to within two leagues of La Castañuela. During the first league we passed Los Ojuelos cattle ranch. Four leagues from this ranch and a quarter of a league to the right of the road one can see La Noria cattle ranch. A little farther on is the Patagalana ranch. The last two leagues of this day's journey are over hills covered with rocks and gullies. Especially noteworthy is a very narrow canyon called El Infiernito because of its jagged cliffs. This precedes by half a league the hacienda of La Castañuela, where we halted. The hacienda is situated on a hill at the mouth of two canyons and its little adobe houses form a plaza. Sixteen guards, including the corporal, are kept there at the expense of the Marqués de San Miguel de Aguayo. They are of great assistance in protecting the haciendas and the camino real, which would be infested by the Natages and Lipanes without this defense.

On the 5th we traveled ten leagues over level land with some pasture. We found nothing noteworthy except two small streams, one at the point of departure, preceding a descent, and the other before reaching Patos. Halfway along the road, on the right and behind a hill, is Macoyu spring. In this vicinity to the south one sees some high mountains forming a chain with the Parras range. At the end and towering above it the Manzanares range stands out. The hacienda has a population of 600 persons of all classes, excluding those in charge of the herds who are sufficient to care for 200,000 head of sheep, cattle, and horses. At this hacienda, cloth, hats, and other articles are manufactured in quantity sufficient for the needs of the servants.

To the Pueblo of San Estevan de Tlaxcala and Villa de Santiago del Saltillo.

On the 6th we traveled sixteen leagues over level ground with some small hills of the same kind as the preceding.

We traveled east for the first eight leagues to San Juan de la Vaquería and Encantada. Two leagues farther on one follows a valley going northeast to the town of Saltillo. One league before that one passes Buenavista rancho. Between it and the settlement there are several more houses. This whole stretch is made up of farm land.

The population is divided into a number of settlements. The pueblo of San Estevan de Tlaxcala is inhabited by pure blood Tlaxcaltecan Indians who founded it during the conquest of this country. And, several colonies have gone out to form the pueblos of Parras, El Alamo, La Monclova, Boca de Leones, and seven others. The total population is three thousand persons. They are governed by a Spanish steward and a governor of their nation and are dependent on the Viceroyalty of Mexico and administered by a Franciscan friar who is their curate. These Indians speak Spanish and are civilized. They possess the best farm lands and orchards of the pleasant plain in which they are situated. The last row of houses in the eastern part of the town and the first row of houses in the Villa de Santiago del Saltillo face each other forming a street. This settlement is quite extensive and is composed of eight thousand persons of all classes, including those who live on neighboring estates. They have their alcalde mayor and two ordinary alcaldes who are heads of their junta or council and subject to the jurisdiction of Nueva Vizcaya, and a parish priest.

To the Hacienda of Anelo.

On the 11th we set out from Saltillo, having stopped for the intervening days to provide ourselves with some necessities for the continuation of our journey. We traveled six leagues north, four of them over level land with many farms and country houses, and the other two over hills covered with loose rocks as far as the hacienda of Santa

María de los Charcos where we halted. In every direction we saw high, bare hills with several passes.

On the 12th we traveled eight leagues principally to the north. At the end of the first league one finds a canyon with a westerly entrance. Several times the canyon turns slightly north and northeast, extending over six leagues. We passed El Convite. Three or four times we crossed a small stream which runs through it. One of its crossings is called Carretas. After going through a small pass at the end one comes out on quite bare land, although there are a number of ravines and some rocks. One league farther is Mesillas hacienda. The footing in the canyon is very difficult, full of stony slopes and washouts. All the surrounding country is arid and there are many bare mountains and hills. Standing out to the east is León mesa a short distance from the wagon road we were following. At its foot runs a much shorter horse trail.

On the 13th we traveled six leagues principally north over level land with some ditches and gullies caused by rain. At the start we crossed the small creek of the preceding day. There is nothing to be noted in all this country as arid and dry as the preceding, except that among the many hills in the area one sights the Sierra Galana to the northwest. It forms a chain with La Paila, which extends west as far as Julimes. At that place there are usually several villages of Lipanes who harass Nueva Vizcaya from there. This night we slept at the Anelo hacienda where the jurisdiction of this province ends and that of Coahuila begins.

JURISDICTION OF THE PROVINCE
OF COAHUILA

To Villa de Santiago de la Monclova.

On the 14th we traveled fourteen leagues principally north-northwest over level land with many mesquites and some pasture, but no water. Halfway along the road to the east is Derrumbaderos, situated at the foot of the ridge called El Espinazo de Ambrosio. Other sierras were visible on all sides. We slept at La Hoya where there is a little house occupied by a family who take care of a well. The water is salty, stinking, and of poor quality.

On the 15th we traveled eighteen leagues north-north-west over level ground with many mesquites and some grass, but no water. We went as far as Castaños hacienda, fourteen leagues away, where there is a spring containing the best water to be found from here to Saltillo. This hacienda is preceded by a rocky ridge of hills. In the four remaining leagues to the town of Santiago de la Monclova there are more rolling hills with many magnetic rocks. In the vicinity there are many high, rugged mountains in every direction.

The map I drew shows the size and arrangement of this town situated, according to my observations, in 27°36′ north latitude and 270°10′ longitude, reckoning from the Tenerife meridian. In it there is a company of thirty-six cavalrymen including the sergeant and two officers. One of the latter is the governor and captain of the company. Their annual allowance is 13,515 pesos, a wasted expense in view of the total uselessness of soldiers in this place and the fact that there is an excess of soldiers on the frontier. There are also a hundred families of settlers including Spaniards, mestizos, and mulattoes. A quarter of a league

142

north of the town, after passing a hill, there is a pueblo
containing fifty-six families of Tlaxcaltecan Indians and
next to it the mission of San Miguel de Aguayo with
twenty-one Cohumeros and Timamares Indians.

To Sauz.

On the 29th, after reviewing this company, we set out
in search of the Santa Rosa presidio. We traveled twelve
leagues north-northeast over level land with occasional
ravines where there are many mesquites, huizaches, etc. In
every direction there were many very high and rugged
ridges. We came to La Casita where we stopped. There
was nothing noteworthy in this stretch except a small creek
midway along the road near the junction of the Coahuila
and Nadadores rivers, and the ruins of several houses on
the banks of the former. These houses were abandoned
for want of water. Opposite La Casita is La Rata sierra
and behind it that of La Candela. The latter range makes
a continuous chain with the Sierra Gorda, of which I shall
speak more at length in another place.

On the 30th we traveled sixteen leagues over level and
well-wooded land with an occasional small hill. A league
and a half beyond our starting place to the northeast is
Baluartes pass in the continuation of the Sierra Madre.
It is formed by two apparently inaccessible flat-topped
hills. The road runs between them through an opening
one eighth of a league wide and half a league long. Three
leagues beyond in the Sandoval pass we forded the Nadadores river in half a *vara* [eighteen inches] of water. This
river rises in springs near El Carmen hacienda situated to
the west of La Casita. The river passes the latter and
winds over a plain. Afterwards it continues north to the
above-mentioned pass and then it joins the Sabinas river
in the direction marked on the map. Five leagues after
crossing the river we came to Santa Cruz where there is a

spring of very good water. We traveled this distance by
varying our route in all the directions of the quadrant until
we finally fixed it to the west. Continuing in this direction
we arrived at Sauz, six leagues away. To the west we had
the continuation of the Sierra Madre running from the
Baluartes pass to Santa Rosa, approximately from south
to north.

JULY

To the Presidio of Santa Rosa.

On the first we traveled eight leagues, the first six northwest over ground like the preceding as far as Los Dolores
hacienda. Two leagues before this we crossed the small
Ibarra pass to enter Santa Rosa valley. It was a very large
plain. The Sabinas river serpentines through the plain. Its
banks are bordered by much cottonwood, ash, and red
cedar and present a beautiful vista. After crossing the dry
arroyos of Los Alamos and Salinas, we arrived at the
hacienda, scarcely two leagues from the Santa Rosa presidio. From this place we traveled southwest over good
pasture land and through occasional thickets as on the preceding day. In the vicinity of this valley, toward east and
north, the Peyotes hills are to be seen in the distance.
Nearby, to the west and south are some sierras of extraordinary height and ruggedness. Many Lipanes live there.
These are known as the sierras of Coahuila and they
extend as far as Julimes, as I have already said.

The map I made shows the shape and arrangement of
Santa Rosa presidio which is situated, according to my
observations, in 28°13′ north latitude, and in 268°49′
longitude. Its garrison consists of a cavalry company of
fifty-two soldiers including three officers and a chaplain.
Its annual allowance amounts to 21,065 pesos. Besides the
families of the soldiers there are forty settlers and several
servants. Twelve ranchos with very good farm lands are

in the neighborhood within a distance of from one to four leagues.

To the Río Grande del Norte.

On the 10th, after the review we set out for San Sabá presidio traveling eight leagues northeast over rolling terrain covered with vegetation. At three leagues we forded the shallow Sabinas river, and after two more leagues the Alamo. We camped at Cenzontle spring three leagues farther on. Nothing was noteworthy except a chain of hills which formed an arc east of Cenzontle. Another ridge beyond a low pass comes out of the Coahuila or Santa Rosa sierras and extends west-northwest.

On the 11th we traveled sixteen leagues generally north by San Joseph, Codorniz passes, and arroyo Laja to San Ildefonso spring. We turned north-northwest to avoid a swamp and went to rancho Patiño. One league farther is an arroyo formed by Escondido spring. Two leagues beyond it is the town of San Fernando where we slept. The population consists of thirty-two families who subsist with difficulty since there is no market for their crops, and the Lipanes, who freely enter this province pretending peace, steal their livestock. For this reason the settlement has not increased since its foundation in 1753. We noted nothing particular in this journey except some low hills.

On the 12th we did not travel. On the 13th we traveled twelve leagues generally north-northeast. At four leagues we crossed the small San Antonio river which joins the Escondido four leagues below, near the road to the Sacramento river, and flows into the Río Grande del Norte ten leagues above San Juan Bautista presidio. At another seven leagues we crossed the San Rodrigo river which empties into the Río Grande two leagues down. We camped on its bank in a thick grove of cottonwoods and alders.

On the 14th we traveled two short leagues northeast over rocky hills. We finally came to a cove which is generally inundated by the river in its greatest rise. The inhabitants call this river the Ancón. We went up river half a league through a forest of shrubs and brambles in search of a small and crudely-made canoe which was at a Lipán ranchería. The canoe was so small and the river so high that we were delayed until the 17th in getting our baggage across. This was accomplished without any misfortune except the death of a Pausan Indian who was carried away by the strong current and drowned without possibility of rescue, and the loss of two horses, drowned on the afternoon of the 16th when the animals were driven into the river to swim across. This stream runs from north-northwest to south-southeast at this crossing where its width is not less than two hundred *toesas* [about 1200 feet].

To the Mission of La Candelaria.

On the 17th we traveled fourteen leagues principally north-northeast over low rocky hills and a wood of mesquites with abundant pasture. At four leagues one comes to the bed of Las Moras arroyo which runs south and is bordered with trees. We found only some puddles of water there. Ten leagues above is the creek's source, called Las Cabeceras del Ojo de las Moras. There we camped. Two leagues before this the road turns west toward this place. Nothing is to be seen in the surroundings on this day's trip except two flat-topped rocks to the north toward which the road runs.

On the 18th we traveled fifteen leagues, nine of them to the arroyo of El Cíbolo, to the north-northeast over long ranges of hills like the preceding. In the vicinity to the east, west, and north, hills and sierras of medium height are visible. Toward the north, half a league from our starting place, are the two flat-topped rocks which served us as a guide on the preceding day. One league to the east of the above-mentioned arroyo there is a pass of medium height from which one descends to the San Joseph valley. Through this pass, commonly called El Cañón, runs the bed of Las Nueces river which is usually dried up. It flows approximately south, along the foot of the opposite hills which form the said valley. The valley's greatest width, east to west, is about a league and a half. Its length, north to south, is probably twelve leagues. In it there are a great many mesquites and thickets and the scarcity of water makes it unsuitable for crops or settlements. We ascended it for five leagues north, as far as La Candelaria where, on the banks of a small arroyo of very fresh and clear water, there was a house with its little chapel and in front of it a large hut constructed by Lipanes. The Fernandine missionaries flattered themselves that they would be able to induce these Indians to live in this place. They never did it and the Lipanes only laughed at the zeal and credulity of the friars.

To the Pueblo of San Lorenzo de la Santa Cruz.

On the 19th we traveled four leagues, the first two and a half north-northeast as far as Las Nueces river. We forded it in very little water but its bed shows how furious its current must be at flood. Taking the road from here to the north we found, at a league and a half, the little pueblo of San Lorenzo de la Santa Cruz, commonly known as the Misión del Cañón. Its origin and progress are similar to those of Candelaria. It merely keeps a detachment of thirty men and an officer from the presidio of San Sabá occupied, and it maintains two useless missionaries. It has no other function than to be a provisioning point for pack-trains which enter with supplies for that presidio. Its shape and bad location are shown on the map I drew of this settlement. Here they have two small three-pounder cannon, one of them with its trunnion broken and both mounted on unserviceable carriages. They are without ball of their caliber or implements for their operation.

To the Presidio of San Sabá.

On the 20th we did not travel. On the 21st we traveled ten leagues north. Half a league up the valley one emerges through a small pass to a wider stretch of ground ending in a league-long canyon among the hills. The Nueces river runs through it and we skirted it, now on one side, now on the other. We crossed it four times before reaching El Cedral where we camped on its bank. All this intervening space and its surroundings are composed of hills and very dense thickets of blackberries, plum, pear and apple trees, and mesquites, cedars, and silver birches intertwined with a great many wild grape vines. A man on horseback can travel this road only with difficulty.

On the 22nd we traveled ten leagues principally north over ground like that of the preceding day but much less thickly wooded with mesquites. In two leagues we came to the source of Las Nueces river in a large spring. Before we reached this spring several other rivers which we had forded the preceding day emptied into the Nueces. One very copious stream, formed from two branches, follows the road the greater part of the way. The road passed through a rocky canyon where several of the rocks were somewhat difficult until it reached the descent to Los Chanes river. On the banks of this river the Chanes nation formerly lived. They now live farther inland. We forded this stream three times and camped on its right bank near a hill thickly covered with trees where there is a little spring of very good water. We noted several sierras and hills around us. Pasture is so abundant that prodigious numbers of buffalos come down to graze during the winter. When hot weather begins they return again to the north.

On the 23rd we traveled ten leagues principally north, although the road makes several deviations from east-northeast to other directions. At the end of four leagues of very rough hills there is a very steep slope. After traveling half a league over a well-wooded plain, one again fords in shallow water Los Chanes river, which flows through a very deep bed. Along its banks there are hills for a distance of three leagues. Then comes a plain two leagues long covered with grass and a variety of trees, among them walnut, wild plum, live-oak, chaparral, mesquite, cedar, etc. Las Lechugas river extends over this same distance. We forded it in shallow water. Half a league farther Las Trancas river unites with Las Lechugas, on whose bank we camped near the junction to the south of us.

On the 24th we traveled eleven leagues principally north-northwest, starting at the ford of the Trancas river, which has to be crossed three times in the four leagues from its source. The latter consists of a spring located on the broken steep slope of a very deep ravine through which it runs. Half a league before this, to the left, is the river or arroyo of San Phelipe. It flows from the northwest, crosses from the other side of the valley we came through, and then continues to the foot of the opposite hills which terminate the valley at a distance of a quarter of a league. A little above the said course where the ravine ends, the road extends north through some hills so low they resemble a plain, and, passing straight through a valley to the north-northwest, seven leagues from the source of the Trancas, it comes to the Abuela arroyo. We forded it and camped on its bank. In this last stretch the country is more open, although there are clumps of trees and some places are made very troublesome by loose rock.

The whole road from El Cañón is exposed to repeated Comanche attacks. Moreover, the danger becomes greater as one approaches the presidio which is constantly watched by the enemy in order to take advantage of any careless-ness or weakness on the part of those who enter or leave, carrying supplies or for other reasons.

On the 25th we traveled two leagues over long ridges of hills covered with very dense tangled woods. For a second time we crossed the Abuela arroyo a short distance from our starting-place. We traveled along it in a northerly direction until we came to the San Sabá river which we crossed in shallow water. Proceeding east for a quarter of a league we came to the presidio. We spent the rest of the day reconnoitering and gathering posts to fence in the horses. We decided to shut them up an hour before day-light as that is the most dangerous time, and turn them loose again after reconnoitering the country.

On the morning of the 26th the scouts reported that they had found the track of five Indians. On this and the preceding day we also noted some smoke signals. We went out that afternoon to reconnoiter the country and sent out scouts to ascertain the origin of the smoke, but they had no news to give on their return.

On the 27th and 28th nothing new happened. We con-tinued to send scouts out and every afternoon we went to explore the countryside.

On the morning of the 29th two scouts came in with a report of having been chased by some Comanches the pre-vious night. On the same morning there was a false alarm caused by the report of a sentinel at one of the advanced posts that he had seen two horses running through the hills half a league away. At the first news the horses were brought into the presidio. Seeing that the enemy did not appear, we went out to reconnoiter. We discovered that it was one of our soldiers who pursued and lassoed a horse which had escaped from the presidio some time before. Having made sure of this, we withdrew and sent two soldiers with two Julimeños Indians to explore the San Juan Lorenzo spring a league and a half away in another direction. They reported on their return, although with some contradiction in their statements, that they had seen three enemy Indians. We went out to verify it that afternoon and discovered it to be false. We found no trace of anything but an old ranchería in the neighborhood of the aforesaid spring.

From the 30th to the fourth of August, the day on which we left for San Antonio de Béjar, nothing particular happened. In the interval I drew the plan of this presidio. Its garrison consists of a cavalry company of one hundred men, including five officers and a chaplain. It is an annual expense of 40,360 pesos to his Majesty and is of no advantage whatever. This I stated in the report which, in fulfillment of an order from his Excellency the Viceroy Marqués de Croix, I sent through the Field Marshal Marqués de Rubí from San Antonio de Béjar, August 12, 1767.

I also repeated my observations and found the place to be situated in 31°38′ north latitude and 273°27′ longitude, reckoning from the Tenerife meridian. Its shape and location are shown in detail on the map. For its defense there are seven small cannon, four of them without trunnions, and all carriages are unserviceable.

AUGUST

To San Antonio de Béjar.

On the 4th we traveled twelve leagues principally southeast with some deviations south-southeast over hills until we came down the Oso valley, eight leagues away. Two leagues before reaching it we had on our right a little spring of water forming a small arroyo and containing only a few puddles. After passing a very deep ravine and crossing a mesa which forms the summit of a hill we went down in a southeasterly direction as far as the little pass of the same name two leagues farther on. In the middle it has an isolated hill which lay to our left. We went through a wide opening between this and some other hills and passed a wood with abundant pasture. In the Cañada del Oso there is a small arroyo with some puddles of water. Two leagues farther on Los Chanes river is again encountered. We crossed it in very little water and camped on its right bank. In the neighborhood many wooded hills are to be seen.

On the 5th we traveled sixteen leagues principally southeast over ground like the preceding. After travelling six leagues we crossed the dry arroyo of La Lajita and two leagues from this, in a valley, is El Almagrito arroyo. Eight leagues farther is Los Pedernales arroyo, as it is commonly called. We camped at its source. Its surroundings are like those of the preceding day. We noticed that the greater part of the hills have flat tops called mesas by the people of the country. The woods covering all this region consist of live-oak, chaparral, and mesquite, and they shelter many herds of buffalos and a large number of bears.

On the afternoon of this day there was a good shower accompanied by a furious wind.

On the 6th we traveled sixteen leagues in a general course over ground like the preceding. At three leagues one passes Los Pedernales river for the third and last time. Five leagues from this is El Mitote arroyo which runs approximately south through a valley where there are some gorges. This arroyo goes approximately four leagues farther to join the Alarcón river, whose course to the east follows the road somewhat apart from it for five leagues. We camped on the left bank.

On the 7th we traveled twelve leagues principally east. The first four leagues we followed the river over level ground with plenty of pasture and trees. We forded the river at the place called Primer Paso. Then comes a very difficult ridge of hills, which grows higher as we approach the little pass of Los Balcones. Two leagues from this is El Rosario arroyo ford. One league beyond is that of Las Moharritas. Another league farther is Atascosito arroyo. Here we began our climb to the pass by an ascending series of hills. From the pass one descends through a pleasant valley covered with much red grass to Los Balcones, two leagues away. This place is so-called because it is a continuation of flat-topped hills overlooking a well-wooded valley. At the foot of these hills is Los Balcones arroyo.

On the 8th we traveled twelve leagues principally southeast. At a short distance from the starting place one crosses Los Balcones arroyo. Two and a half leagues from there Los Alamitos arroyo is crossed. It is one half the distance to the little pass where there is a small arroyo. Up to this arroyo the ground is level with abundant pasture and some clumps of live-oaks, chaparral, etc. In the neighborhood there are many gentle hills where woods, of the same kind as the preceding, are thicker. Seven leagues from the pass is San Antonio de Béjar. Two leagues before it there are a number of hills. All that ground and its surroundings are of the same character as the preceding, although there are more mesquite woods as soon as one descends to the plain. There is nothing else to be mentioned except El León arroyo which we found dry half-way along the road, and San Antonio river, which we forded a quarter of a league from the town.

DESCRIPTION OF THE KINGDOM OF
NUEVA ESTREMADURA OR PROVINCE
OF COAHUILA

This province is situated between 26° and 32° north latitude including the presidio of San Sabá, although the latter is excluded from its jurisdiction. It is between 262° and 275° longitude counting from the first meridian which passes through the Theide peak on the Island of Santa Cruz de Tenerife. It is bounded on the east and south by the New Kingdom of León, along the arroyo of La Pendencia; on the east by the colony of Nuevo Santander; between east and north by the province of Texas on the Medina river, which serves as a dividing line from its origin until its union with the San Antonio river; on the north by the Apaches, Lipanes, and Natages who dwell on the banks of the Río Grande del Norte and in the adjoining mountains; on the west by Nueva Vizcaya, whose jurisdiction extends to but does not include the presidio at the junction of the Conchas and Norte rivers; and on the south as far as the junction of the Saltillo river.

The settlements are reduced to the three small towns of Santiago de la Monclova, San Fernando de Austria, and San Pedro de Gigedo, two pueblos, and several haciendas where there are 777 families of Spaniards, mestizos, and mulattoes. This number includes the men of the three companies of the presidios of Monclova, Santa Rosa, and San Juan Bautista del Río Grande. There are also nine missions where the Franciscan fathers minister to 382 Indian families of the Terocodames, Pacpoles, Tacquites, Ocanes, Payaguanes, Cíbolos, Canos, Ostujanes, Pachoches, Apes, Colorados, Obayás, Tobosos, Xixames, Silangayas, Sadujanes, Siguares, Pitas, Pacuafin, Pajalatames, Carrizos, Conhumeros, Timamares, Pampopas, Tilixais, Mescales, Borrados, Pausanes, Manos de Perro, Piguiques, and Julimeños nations. There are, in addition, 126 families of Tlaxcaltecan Indians who live in two pueblos.

The climate is mild, although sometimes inclined to be hot. The country is mountainous. In the valleys between the mountains are the settlements and haciendas where every kind of grain is raised in abundance, and in addition horses, mules, cattle, and sheep. The sierras, which are very high and broken, provide plentiful wood. All species of animals and birds common to the other provinces live in these mountains. There are also several kinds of fish in the Nadadores, Sabinas, Río Grande del Norte, Las Nueces, and El Frío rivers and also the San Antonio, San Rodrigo, San Diego rivers and other smaller streams which flow through this district.

This province is now apparently at peace with the Lipán and Natage Apache Indians who live in its confines on the banks of the Río Grande, El Colorado, and El Puerco [Pecos]. Nevertheless, it does not seem to me superfluous to describe the places which they most commonly frequent in these vicinities for the purpose of committing robberies in this province and Nueva Vizcaya. Should they someday determine to make war upon these two provinces, defense of these places would be the best or only means of safety for their inhabitants, whose ruin would otherwise be inevitable.

The places where, despite the peace, the Apaches attack shepherds and cattle herders of the haciendas of Sardinas and Quatro Ciénegas and run off their mules and horses, are the sierra of San Blas, the sierras near La Salada pass, Sacramento pass, at the mouth of the three rivers, at San Marcos, and at Tora pass. From these places they also cross over to Vizcaya, overrunning the Sierra Galana, that

of Acatita de Baján, and the Cerro Colorado. In all the
country extending from the southwest to the northwest, in
respect to Monclova, besides the places named, their chief
route is by the sierra of Quatro Ciénegas and its cañon, and
the passes of Las Calaveras, Agua Verde, Santa Catarina,
El Thenaute, El Carrizalejo, El Zacate de Enjalma, Los
Berrendos plain, El Potrero de Padilla, El Capulín, and
the Boca del Aura. Those which they frequent in order to
attack the neighborhood of Santa Rosa and the Sabinas
river are by the *boca* or pass of Santa Ana where Los Alamos river has its source, by the Potrero de la Babia, and
an infinite number of other places in the immense mountain
chain lying between the north and west of the aforesaid
presidio. There are a number of valleys in which are situated the springs of San Joseph, Santa María del Socorro,
San Andrés, La Nutria, and others at a distance of a regular day's journey apart, until one comes to the crossing of
the Río Grande at San Vicente or Santa Rita. From this
place one continues to the presidio of La Junta de los Ríos.
Since the country lying between this presidio and that of
Santa Rosa is little known, making its passage difficult, and
is supposed to lack water, I am going to reproduce the
itinerary followed by the Governor of Coahuila, Don
Pedro de Rábago y Terán, who, by superior order, made
an exploration of this interv ning country. It would not
only be conducive but indispensable to locate a presidio
here in order to clean out that uninhabited pocket which
is the refuge of all who commit rascalities from that side
in Nueva Vizcaya and Coahuila. Not only the enemies hide
in it, but also apostates and thieves from many neighboring missions. From here they sally out to rob and kill pass-
ersby. Since this matter has been treated widely and dif-
fusely in my plan for guarding Nueva Vizcaya from enemy
attacks, I shall refer to what is said in it and go on to record
the itinerary as I have promised.

Route followed by Don Pedro de Rábago y Terán.

The governor mentioned above set out from the presidio of Santa Rosa with a suitable detachment, and, taking the road to the west, traveled five leagues, halting at El Cura arroyo.

On the 2nd day he traveled five more leagues in the same direction, halting at La Cabecera, or head of the Escondido arroyo.

On the 3rd day he traveled six leagues in the same direction and stopped at the place called La Rosa de San Juan.

On the 4th he traveled five leagues in the same direction as far as Cabezones.

On the 5th he traveled to the Potrero and La Babia spring eight leagues farther in the same direction.

On the 6th he halted at Los Cerritos seven leagues away and in the same direction.

On the 7th he traveled nine leagues in the same direction, stopping at San Xavier.

On the 8th he ascended a hill and halted on the top, having traveled three leagues in the preceding direction.

On the 9th he traveled seven leagues in the same direction and halted at San Pedro.

On the 10th he traveled six leagues in the same direction and halted at Santa María.

On the 11th he went to the San Ramón pools, traveling six leagues north.

On the 12th he traveled ten leagues in the same direction and halted on the bank of the Río Grande del Norte, crossing it at the pass or ford of San Vicente.

On the 13th he traveled four leagues in the preceding direction and halted at El Barrial spring.

On the 14th he traveled five leagues west until he came to the Basilio waterhole.

On the 15th he traveled five leagues in the same direction as far as Las Calabazas.

On the 16th he traveled six leagues in the preceding direction to La Concepción.

On the 17th he traveled five leagues in the same direction to La Muralla de San Dalmacio, which is a very high cliff facing the Río Grande. The river from that place enters a very deep and narrow canyon which cuts through a very lofty mountain range.

On the 18th he traveled four leagues north, stopping at La Nutria arroyo.

On the 19th he traveled seven leagues west, stopping at La . . . [missing].

On the 20th he traveled six leagues in the same direction to San Cristóbal.

On the 21st he traveled five leagues in the preceding direction as far as Los Chupaderos.

On the 22nd he traveled seven leagues north to the arroyo Colorado.

On the 23rd he traveled six leagues west to La Mula.

On the 24th he traveled seven leagues in the same direction until he reached the presidio of La Junta and the Guadalupe pueblo, having traveled in all 144 leagues.

On his return he came on the first day to El Alamo, seven leagues away, having crossed the river at Los Puliques pueblo.

On the second day he traveled eight leagues, halting at Los Encinos.

On the third he traveled seven leagues to the headwaters of La Nutria arroyo.

On the 4th he went to La Hedionda, a distance of nine leagues.

On the 5th to the San Vicente pass, eighteen leagues away. He traveled the whole forty-eight leagues to the east.

From this place he retraced his route by the same watering places passed in his journey from Santa Rosa. This road is shorter than the preceding, for they traveled only 125 leagues and might have shortened it still more. The Julimes Indians, who are well acquainted with this country, assert that it is only eighty leagues.

JURISDICTION OF TEXAS

The town and presidio of San Antonio de Béjar are located, according to my observation, in 29°52' north latitude and in 275°57' longitude, reckoning by the Tenerife meridian. Their plan and size are shown in the map I drew. The number of inhabitants is only sixteen families from the Canaries who came to form this settlement, transported at his Majesty's expense; some of their servants, and a company of twenty-two men, including the captain and a sergeant. The allowance for the company amounts annually to 8,595 pesos. The King also pays 450 pesos a year to a parish priest who ministers to them.

Following the course of the river for three leagues one comes to the five missions: San Antonio de Valero, La Purísima Concepción, San Joseph de Aguayo, San Juan Capistrano, and San Francisco de la Espada. They are situated on both sides of the river and inhabited by 809 Indians of the Payayas, Sarames, Chanes, Cocos, Pajalates, Tecamos, Pampopas, Mesquites, Aguastayas, Pamacas, Chayopines, Pacaos, Venados, Borrados, Patas de Perro, and others. They are administered by ten Franciscan fathers of La Cruz de Querétaro and Nuestra Señora de Guadalupe de Zacatecas, with 450 pesos each annually paid by the royal treasury. This expense could be avoided entirely for these missions are rich. Moreover, they could greatly reduce the number of ministers who uselessly employ as guards fourteen or fifteen soldiers from the San Antonio company. The docility of the Indians and their one hundred bow and arrow men place them beyond reach of any local or outside attack. The useless employment of the soldiers leaves San Antonio entirely abandoned, its garrison completely dispersed among these stations, and the care of its horses made impossible for any operation because the reverend fathers refuse to give a helping hand with their Indians. Consequently the enemies are continually committing outrages in this vicinity.

To the Colorado River.

On the 25th we set out for Los Adaes presidio. We traveled twelve leagues principally east southeast over fairly level ground well-wooded with mesquites, live-oaks, and walnut trees. At four leagues we crossed the Salado arroyo in shallow water. Four leagues farther is Las Calaveras where the Aguila arroyo flows in a bed so deep and rugged that only occasionally can one reach the water. Four leagues beyond this we camped at Los Chayopines on the left bank of the San Antonio river which we forded when we left. This river had already been united with the Medina river whose junction, on its right bank, is nine leagues west of the presidio. Half a league below, the Salado creek flows into it, and one league before our stopping place the Aguila joins it. Both enter on the left bank and the course then winds to the south.

On the 26th we traveled fifteen leagues in the same direction, but through country less wooded, with occasional live-oaks and a great deal of red grass. At seven leagues we crossed the Marcelino arroyo, which has only a few pools of water. Two leagues farther was El Cíbolo, on whose banks are the rancho San Bartolo and several others belonging to the settlers of San Antonio. Some seasonal corn is sown and they raise some horses and mules. Up to now they have suffered no annoyance from the enemies. Six leagues farther is the Cleto arroyo, with some puddles of water. Here we camped. All these arroyos empty into the San Antonio river on our right.

On the 27th we traveled fourteen leagues principally northeast over ground like the preceding. At six leagues is

El Cuchillo arroyo, formed by three small streams like the preceding. I should say that they unite a short distance from where we crossed. All empty into the San Antonio river below Bahía. Eight leagues from the latter we crossed the Guadalupe river at El Governador ford in water up to a horse's belly. It is so rapid, on account of the narrowness of its bed, that after a light rain it becomes impassable except on rafts. At this place it runs in a south-southeast direction. Its banks are covered with a dense growth of trees entangled with vines. The whole width of the valley is inundated by the river at flood time. We camped on its left bank outside the woods.

On the 28th we traveled thirteen leagues principally north-northeast over ground like the preceding with some clumps of live-oaks and immense forests of the same trees in every direction. At four leagues is El Cuervo arroyo. Six leagues beyond is that of El Rosal. A league farther is the arroyo or bog of Padre Campa. At a league and a half one passes Los Ramitos arroyo and half a league beyond this flows the arroyo of San Estevan where we camped. Several of these arroyos dry up. Others retain some puddles, but all rise rapidly in rainy season.

On the 29th we traveled eighteen leagues north-north-east to La Navidad arroyo over ground like the preceding. In the ten league interval and one league from our start, we reached La Vaca arroyo. Three leagues from this we came to the Breviario arroyo, and at six leagues La Navidad. In this last distance some other smaller nameless creeks are omitted. Turning here to the northeast, we came at seven leagues to Los Cedritos arroyo, running through a deep ravine, preceded by a thick wood of live-oaks. This wood continues also on the other side as far as the Colorado river one league away. The undergrowth becomes thicker as one draws nearer and on both banks there are giant cottonwoods and so many wild grapevines and various kinds of bushes that it is impenetrable. It is even difficult to pass by the highway, now reduced to a bad, narrow path with limbs of trees lying across it which one has to dodge. We finally forded this river in water up to the horses' shoulders. We camped on its left bank beyond the belt of woods on its edges.

To the Trinity River.

On the 30th we traveled fourteen leagues principally north-northeast through woods as far as El Azúcar arroyo three leagues away. We traveled over rough ground like that of the preceding days with some clumps and woods of live-oaks in sight. After two more leagues we passed El Azúcar arroyo, then La Sandía, and two farther on the Piltonte arroyo. Three leagues from this is the Juana Guerra arroyo. Finally four leagues beyond is the Bernabé on whose banks we camped. All these creeks are of the same character as the preceding.

On the 31st we traveled thirteen leagues principally north-northeast over ground with more woods than that of the preceding days. At four leagues we crossed Corral de Barrancas creek and after two more leagues the Quita Calzones. Then we followed for a space of three leagues thick live-oak woods as far as Don Carlos arroyo. Through this wood, with some open spaces, it is two leagues to the first clear spot where there is an arroyo with some puddles. The two succeeding leagues intervening between this and the second clear space are of the same character and in this open spot is another arroyo. In both places it is difficult for the horses to drink because of the depth of the pools and waterholes. Here we camped on a small plain, a natural clearing in the middle of the wood, called by the natives of the country *placeta*.

September

On the 1st day we traveled ten leagues principally north through a thick wood of white cottonwoods, walnut trees, plums, medlars, and other kinds of trees, with some open spaces. In the first league of this journey we forded, in shallow water, the first branch of the river called Brazos de Dios. A league and a half farther we crossed the second arm at a short distance from its junction. Two leagues and a half from it we camped at a place called El País.

The pagan Jaramanes Indians live in a territory lying between the Colorado and the Brazos de Dios and extending to the Gulf of Mexico. Although these Indians are little to be feared, one must use caution when traveling through their territory because they habitually steal horses from travelers.

On the 2nd we traveled thirteen leagues principally north-northeast. The road runs through open spaces crossed by belts of live-oaks. In all this vicinity the growth of trees is very thick. At eight leagues we crossed the Corpus Christi arroyo in shallow water. It is preceded by another nameless stream which flows in a very deep bed. Turning from the first-named to the east, at a little more than four leagues, we came to Navas Soto creek, which is followed by a quarter of a league of woods. There are no more arroyos as far as Navas Soto lagoon where we camped among some gentle hills.

On the 3rd we traveled twenty-two leagues principally northeast over ground like that of the preceding day. We went as far as the small El Francés lagoon which is in the midst of a thick wood twelve leagues distant. It is preceded by El Carrizo arroyo. One league from the above-mentioned lagoon is Caimán lagoon of the same size. The road runs through a wood which is much thicker and has some clearings considerably smaller than the preceding. The road continues in this way to the Trinity river. Seven leagues from the last lagoon one encounters the arroyo called El Atascoso. From here the road deviates north in order to reach the ford of the Trinity river. We could not cross it having arrived very late and because the wood on its banks is nearly impenetrable. So we camped on this side and it immediately began to rain and continued violently the whole night.

To the Missions of Nacogdoches and Los Ais.

On the 4th, rain continued with some interruptions until afternoon. The ground where we were camped became so swampy that we were compelled to set out. We crossed the Trinidad river over a stone ledge which extends across its entire width. There was scarcely a span of water. We had no difficulty except at the channels on each side which become very bad in rainy season and which are very swift and high because of the depth of the bed on both sides. This difficulty overcome, we set our course north-northeast over hills covered with a thick woods of live-oak, common oak, walnut trees, and pine, and interlaced with many grape vines. We came to the arroyo of El Chicharrón a little before that of Santa Efigenia, six and a half leagues away. Farther on is the site of Las Peñitas. We camped on a hill. At its foot was a small perennial stream.

On the 5th we traveled fifteen leagues principally northeast over ground like that of the preceding day. At two leagues we crossed Las Castañas arroyo, and two more that of Santa Coleta. Four leagues from the latter, at San Pedro, are the majority of the Texas Indian rancherías. They are our friends and are spread throughout that vicinity occupying the plain which extends to the Nechas river three leagues away. We forded this river in shallow water and one league beyond we climbed a hill. On the summit is a mound which appears to be hand-made. Here it

was that the conquerors found the main body of this nation
with whom they formed a friendship which has been preserved inviolate.

On the 6th we traveled twelve leagues principally east-
northeast over ground like the preceding, although more
troublesome, because of the gravel and many tree-trunks
and roots lying across the road. At four leagues we crossed
the Angelina arroyo and at another four that of El Con-
ductor. Four leagues farther on we arrived at the Mission
of Nacogdoches where we found only one Franciscan friar
from Nuestra Señora de Guadalupe de Zacatecas, two soldiers with their families, and some young farm workers.
The priest had not one Indian to whom he could minister,
nor had there been one during more than the forty years
of this mission's existence. On the 6th [sic] we did not
travel.

On the 7th we traveled three leagues east-southeast over
ground like the preceding. We crossed La Nana arroyo at
a quarter of a league and one and three quarters of a
league farther that of El Carrizo. One league beyond this
we camped on the banks of the Atascoso. In all these arroyos there were only a few pools of water.

On the 8th we traveled fourteen leagues east through
country like the preceding. At six leagues we crossed the
arroyo of Las Amoladeras and in another league that of
Atoyaque. Five leagues from the latter the mission of Los
Ais is situated on a small hill near an arroyo. This mission
is about as useless as the preceding one but the disadvan-
tage is greater to his Majesty for the reason that two
priests are maintained in it with an annual salary of 450
pesos each. There are also a lay brother and two soldiers
with their families who compose the entire population. The
Ais Indian nation lives in the neighborhood. They speak
Spanish well and appeal to the padres only when they want

something. Two leagues farther there is a spring called El Palo Gacho, where we camped.

To the Presidio of Nuestra Señora del Pilar de los Adaes.

On the 9th we traveled sixteen leagues, the first eleven east-northeast, and the remainder to the north-northeast, over ground like the preceding. At the end of the first two leagues we crossed El Lobanillo arroyo where the missionaries of Ais had a rancho which they themselves are believed to have ordered to be burned. At two more leagues there is another arroyo without a name, and three leagues from it is the site called La Cuesta Alta. Two more farther on is El Patrón arroyo and two from this to the east-southeast is the Sabinas river which we forded in shallow water. During the rainy season it overflows its banks and widens out about four leagues. Finally, after traveling five leagues from the ford, we camped on the banks of Las Cabezas arroyo, which gives its name to a small plain nearby.

On the 10th we traveled twelve leagues east-northeast through country like the preceding. At the end of the first two leagues we crossed a dry arroyo called El Vallecito, and three leagues beyond that El Cautivo arroyo. In three more we reached Los Tres Llanos rancho. One league from this is another of the same name, and half a league before arriving at the presidio of Nuestra Señora del Pilar de los Adaes one crosses the arroyo Hondo.

This presidio is situated, according to my observation, in 32°15′ north latitude and in 285°52′ longitude, reckoning from the Tenerife meridian. Its fortification and plan will be seen on the map I made with the note that the irregular stockade forming its enclosure is rotten and in ruins. The garrison consists of a cavalry company of sixty men, including the lieutenant-ensign, sergeant, and governor, who is their commandant. The salary of the latter is

2,500 pesos annually, which, added to the amount of the pay of the company, amounts to 27,765 pesos yearly.

Annexed to the presidio is the mission San Miguel de Cuéllar de los Adaes, with two priests of the same order as the preceding who serve only to minister to the presidio, for the Indians who give their name to this country are of the same character and as irreducible as the others.

To Rancho El Atascoso.

On the 28th we set out for the presidio of Orcoquizac, retracing our steps to Nacogdoches by the same route. We arrived there on the first of October, having traveled a distance of forty-five leagues.

OCTOBER

On the 2nd we traveled five leagues to the south along a middle course over ground like the preceding. At a quarter of a league from the mission we crossed the Nana arroyo. In the interval between it and the Angelina river, which runs southwest, we passed another nameless mission. Fording the river in shallow water we camped on its left bank. In flood time it rushes from its bed furiously and covers a flat which lies between two hills a quarter of a league apart. This flat is called Las Lagunas.

On the 3rd we traveled twelve leagues south one-quarter southeast, over more extended hills and thinner woods with more clearings than on preceding days. At ten leagues we crossed the small Los Vidais arroyo. Nearby were some huts, deserted but in good condition, where a group of the Vidais nation was living. Two leagues farther we camped on the left bank of the Neches river. In this region it flows east in a very deep bed although there is little water. With but few intermissions all this day and the following night, it rained.

On the 4th we traveled ten leagues south-southwest over
land like the preceding. At three leagues we crossed San
Cayetano arroyo, and seven leagues beyond we came to
another without a name. We camped nearby on a hill
which we named San Francisco because we arrived there
on that Saint's day.

On the 5th we traveled twelve leagues southwest along
a middle course over ground like the preceding. At four
leagues is La Parida. For the eight remaining leagues we
traveled through thick woods that were almost impenetrable on account of the great amount of chaparral which
chokes up that narrow path. The way is obstructed by
fallen trees and branches lying across it, making passage
very difficult because one has to avoid the brush and climb
over the trunks. To this inconvenience another was added.
At intervals the rain fell all day until five in the afternoon.
At that hour the downfall became steady and the road impracticable, and we were forced to make camp on an almost
imperceptible and nameless rise. It was close to a swamp
where there was plenty of red grass into which we turned
the horses. Three leagues before arriving at this place we
passed El Purgatorio arroyo, preceded by several others
without names.

On the 6th we were delayed by the furious rain-storm
which began the day before and continued almost without
stopping nearly all of today.

On the 7th we traveled seven short leagues south one
quarter southeast over ground like the preceding, but so
swampy and full of water that it was difficult to travel over
it. At the end of the first four leagues we came to an arroyo
running southwest. We were able to ford it notwithstanding it was running full. A quarter of a league from it we
crossed, with our baggage on our shoulders, the Santa Gertrudis arroyo which also flows southwest. A tree across the
creek's bed served us as a bridge. The animals swam over

at a point a little above where it unites with the first-mentioned arroyo. Traveling afterwards for a short league through a wood so full of water that it formed a lagoon, we camped in the driest clear space we could find.

On the 8th we traveled fourteen leagues along a general course between south and one quarter southeast. At four leagues we came to the plain and site of Los Tepalcates, and at another four to El Alamo. This is wooded country with several clearings where there is no lack of water. Two leagues from this place beyond the canyon formed by some low and more open hills, we entered Guajolote plain. When it rains this plain becomes a lake, at times impassable, the water reaching to a man's waist and to the horse's belly. We traveled for four leagues to a small rancho at a place called El Atascoso. Here we camped. Extraordinary features of this plain are flat-topped mounds, from four to six *varas* in diameter and from one to two in height, which nature has scattered about in great number making it passable. Rising above the surface of the water they serve as a resting-place for the people who often have to carry their goods on their shoulders because the beasts become worn out, or lack food. On these mounds they can keep their feet dry while packing the loads which otherwise would be almost impossible.

To Presidio San Luis de Ahumada or Orcoquizac.

On the 9th we traveled ten leagues principally south, although the road makes a semi-circle to avoid the lagoon formed by the Trinidad river, which lay two leagues to our right all day. At the end of the first four leagues over level swampy ground like that of Guajolote, we crossed the Calzones arroyo which flows west and empties into the Trinidad river. Leaving behind us Los Horconcitos we forded El Piélago arroyo in water up to the horses' bellies. It also runs west and empties, like the Calzones, into the aforesaid

river. Both overflow in rainy season and inundate the six
leagues lying between the last-named and the presidio of
San Luis de Ahumada, commonly known as Orcoquizac.
This country is well-wooded but has many clearings. In the
first-named, from the beginning of Guajolote plain, there
are plenty of rushes and coarse grass on hilltops where
many trees are growing.

The map I drew shows the size of this presidio, located
according to my observations in 30°23′ north latitude and
283°52′ longitude, counting from the Tenerife meridian.
It is situated in the country belonging to the Orcoquizac
Indian nation which is one league from the Gulf of Mexico
in an easterly direction and five leagues on the south from
the mouth of the river. After it flows a quarter of a league
west of the presidio it becomes very wide and deep, its low
banks damming it up. A sandbank closes its mouth and
stops its flow. Thus the entire country is full of lagoons
which prevent one from traveling along its banks. These
lagoons also occur in the east; hence it is necessary to make
a ten-league detour to reach the sea. We accomplished this
with many difficulties and the loss of many horses. The
whole coast is similar as far as La Balise, belonging to
Louisiana. This is near the mouth of the Mississippi river
and therefore impassable.

The garrison of this presidio consists of a cavalry company of thirty-one men, including captain, lieutenant, and
sergeant. Its annual cost is 13,245 pesos. Nine hundred
pesos is the allotment of the two Franciscan friars who
minister to the troop and the adjoining mission of Nuestra
Señora de la Luz. Here the same conditions prevail as at
the preceding missions. I therefore consider this presidio
useless since it does not serve the missions. The latter are
of no use because of the slight inclination of those natives
to embrace our holy religion, a fact clearly evident since
the year 1758 when the only mission was founded there. In

all this time not a single Indian has been converted. Still less can be said for the other reasons of state which were advanced for its establishment. We can sacrifice a certain Monsieur Lampin who traded in a few hides on that uninhabitable coast, secure in his belief that no nation would attempt to form a colony there, especially in the place where the presidio is situated. It is very unhealthy and in the midst of lagoons which make communication impossible with any other of our settlements. For this reason as well as poor management, those unhappy people are compelled to live the greater part of the year on roots called sweet potatoes, medlars, nuts, plums, and chestnuts smaller than those of Spain, and other wild fruits. This is the customary diet of those natives whose laziness makes them content with it rather than trouble to hunt deer and bear, of which there is an abundance. They depend, for their final recourse, upon the lagoon, where there are many fish which they harpoon. Alligators also abound there. The Indians play with them, catching them by the snout and dragging them to shore where they kill them.

To the Colorado River.

On the 16th, after the review of this company had been concluded, we set out crossing the Trinidad river by canoe at the place where the lagoon joins it. At this point it has a width of eighty *toesas* and three and a half *toesas* in its greatest depth. Turning northwest we traveled four leagues over level ground covered with reeds, tule, and coarse grass and having the river on our right. On the left we had a channel which runs out of the river about three leagues farther up and is called Cayo by the natives. Both river and channel are bordered by many trees outlining their course through an otherwise barren plain. We crossed the last-named river on a bridge constructed as a precaution and passed through a wooded spot which follows. We came to another clearing which extended to the place on the road where we camped on a small hill after crossing a creek on another small bridge. The hill was covered with live-oaks. During this whole day's journey we found no more than a miry place here and there and a few puddles in the hollows. In the rainy season, however, the whole plain forms an impassable lagoon.

On the 17th we traveled eight leagues west-northwest beginning at Caramanchel plain where we found swamp-land. It is worse in rainy season than the preceding since, besides rain-water, it is flooded by an arroyo of the same name which has no outlet. We forded it after traveling six and a half leagues. Continuing over the San Jacinto plain which we found similar to the preceding, we arrived at the river of this same name. We all crossed it on a raft with the best of our baggage, leaving the rest on our mules in order that they might be able to keep their footing. We camped on the left bank [*sic*] in a wooded stretch which lines both sides. The mosquitoes were so rabid that it was impossible for us to rest or sleep the whole night. Both banks are clear of obstructions and in the distance on all sides are thick oak groves. The intervening space is covered with coarse grass, tule, etc., like the preceding.

On the 18th we traveled nine leagues along a similar course over level land. At the start, for two leagues, one travels through a very thick woods with swampy soil, called La Lagunilla. Afterwards the ground becomes better and there were several clearings. We crossed El Gallo plain, with its several swamps. At five leagues we also crossed, on a small wooden bridge, El Gallo arroyo. It has little water but is very miry. Continuing for two leagues over another plain the same as this, we reached the Sabinas arroyo. With our baggage on our shoulders, we crossed the arroyo on a tree which had been cut down for this purpose. We camped at a gunshot from its bank, where the wood, which is very thick in that neighborhood, begins to clear. We left the horses on the opposite side because the pasture and conditions for guarding them were better. This arroyo runs north and after several windings empties into San Jacinto arroyo.

On the 19th we traveled thirteen leagues west one quarter northwest, crossing a bare plain with many ponds and swamps until we came to its termination, La Rifa arroyo, five leagues away. The plain is named after the arroyo. After crossing the plain we entered another like it and traveled over it as far as Santa Rosa arroyo three leagues away. A quarter of a league before this some low hills begin and continue for five leagues up to San Isidro arroyo. On the slopes of these hills two unnamed rivulets flow and there are some ravines with a number of pools and an occasional swamp in the hollows. We crossed this last arroyo in shallow water and camped on a little hill at whose foot another arroyo unites with the former. In the vicinity of this day's journey, the same as in those of the preceding days, the view is limited by an immense and continuous live-oak thicket. In the clearings one finds only red grass, tule, reeds, and reed grass.

On the 20th we traveled thirteen leagues west, the first six by La Magdalena plain which is similar to those preceding. At its extremity an arroyo runs through the middle of a belt of live-oaks. It has its rise in two springs which give their name to the plain and unite near the place where we crossed. Four leagues farther on we forded the river of Los Brazos de Dios on a bottom of flat stone, in water reaching to the holsters of our pistols. Its width, measured straight across, was not less than fifty *toesas* but it was increased by the obliqueness of the crossing. The passage is made quite dangerous by the narrowness of the channel and the violence of the current which flows south. On the other side, in a wood half a league long, we came to a lagoon which forms when this river is in flood. We were able to cross it, but with a great deal of trouble, the water rising almost to the horses' backs. Afterwards we entered El Barril plain in which numerous swamps made passage very difficult. At last, with an immense amount of trouble, we reached a small hill which terminates the plain. We traveled a league over gentle hills until reaching the Mota de Viperina, where we camped. The surroundings are the same as the preceding except that the river banks are much more densely wooded. Under cover of this thick growth the Jaramanes Indians frequently steal horses, taking advantage of the carelessness of travelers, as I have said in another place.

On the 21st we traveled eight leagues midway to the west-northwest. After three leagues of ground composed of hills higher than those of the previous day, we came to a small arroyo called La Caja, and an eighth of a league beyond was that of San Sebastián. From this point we traveled over moderately level land as far as La Zorilla five leagues away, where we camped after a difficult crossing of some swamps in the intervening space. Nevertheless, in regard to footing and pasture, this part of the country is much better than the preceding. The woods in this vicinity are of the same character as before.

On the 22nd it rained nearly all morning. Nevertheless we started, although somewhat late. Proceeding west-southwest we traveled nine leagues over a long range of hills. At two leagues from the wood we came to a clear space, where the short arroyo of El Tapestle flows. One league from this is Las Peñitas arroyo and in another league that of Bernabé. In the last two leagues the clear spaces alternated with woods of live-oaks where the ground underfoot is quite swampy, especially on the slopes. At five leagues is Juana Rosa arroyo. This country is more open and clear, but with more than enough mud and mire.

Three quarters of a league before reaching the last arroyo we again struck the road we took in our entrance.

On the 23rd, retracing our way through the places I have already mentioned we reached the Colorado river after traveling a distance of ten leagues. We employed the rest of the day in getting out a canoe which was submerged on the other side. For this purpose we had some men swim across.

On the 24th in the morning the canoe was finally taken out and repaired, and in the afternoon people and baggage began to cross over.

On the 25th nearly everything had crossed over with the exception of some trifles which were transported early on the following day. The horses and mules were then driven in to swim. Because of thick growth on the banks, which impeded their landing, we lost seven animals.

To the Presidio of Nuestra Señora de Loreto.

On the 26th we traveled to the place known as El Breviario, fourteen leagues away.

On the 27th to El Rosal, distant seven leagues.

On the 28th to the Guadalupe river ten leagues away. Since this stream was very high we went down two leagues along its course. It forms a semi-circle at the place called El Piélago and continues east at the place where we had to cross in a small and inferior canoe, constructed in anticipation by the soldiers of La Bahía. It was so likely to overturn that we added some tree trunks to it, in order to use it with a margin of security. The day passed in this work and in beginning another and larger canoe. Although we worked all night, it was not possible to launch the canoe until eleven the following morning. Then it was found to be so heavy and likely to sink, on account of the green wood, that we preferred to use the old one.

On the 29th the greater part of the people and baggage crossed over in the two canoes.

On the 30th the rest crossed and we set out traveling ten leagues south over gentle hills where the trees were considerably thinner and gradually diminished. We crossed several arroyos on the slopes of these hills which came in succession as follows: Las Moharras, El Bagre, Las Cruces, La Cabecera or the source of El Perdido. Here we camped on a small elevated spot in a clump of live-oaks.

On the 31st we traveled three leagues south one quarter southwest over ground like the preceding though somewhat more open. After two leagues we arrived at Salsipuedes arroyo, which is immediately followed by a clump of trees called La Monaguilla one league away from the presidio of Nuestra Señora de Loreto. One eighth of a league before reaching it we crossed the San Antonio river in a canoe at a point near the Espíritu Santo mission.

The map I drew of the aforesaid presidio and surroundings shows its size and plan. According to my observations it is situated in 29°39' north latitude and in 277°54' longitude, reckoning from the Tenerife meridian, fifteen leagues from the coast of the Gulf of Mexico, considering that this distance is geometrically measured between east and south. Proximity to the Gulf gives it the same bad climate. There is a strong tendency toward scurvy and a great many people die of it. Few escape malaria in any year.

By the shortest and most accessible road to the coast it is twenty leagues. In rainy season it is impassable. The lagoons of Lampazos, San Nicolás, and others which are from six to eight leagues away from the presidio overflow and form several arms and outlets. These empty into the bays, cut off the roads, and render any ford impassable.

The cavalry company which garrisons this presidio is composed of fifty soldiers, including three officers and a

sergeant. They cost his Majesty 19,280 pesos annually.
Besides the troop there are forty-six settlers, among whom
may be collected sixteen guns, although one can count but
little on them because they are necessarily absent the
greater part of the time earning a living. In the vicinity
there are two missions. That of Espíritu Santo was
founded on the second of May, 1727, for some Cocos Indians. Afterwards they abandoned it and retreated to the
coast where they live in heathenism and cause some damage to the Spaniards. For this reason the mission was repopulated with Jaramanes and Tamiques who followed
the example of their predecessors. Only twenty-three families, comprising thirty-nine persons — I should say ninety-
three persons — remain there. To the west of the presidio,
two leagues up river on the right bank the mission of
Nuestra Señora del Rosario is situated. It was founded
in the year 1758, with the Indian nations of Cojanes,
Guapites, and Carancauces. Of these there now exist only
seventy-one baptized persons and thirty savages, many
more having escaped to live at liberty with their relatives.
The two missions are in charge of three Franciscan fathers
from the colleges of Guadalupe de Zacatecas and Santa
Cruz de Querétaro, each of the friars enjoying an annual
stipend of 450 pesos paid by his Majesty.

NOVEMBER

To Villa de Laredo.

On the 12th, having finished the review of this presidio,
we set out for that of San Juan Bautista del Río Grande
del Norte. We traveled ten leagues west over gentle hills
with abundant pasture and some clumps of trees. They are
covered with cattle, some of the herds belonging to the
missions, some to the deceased captain, some to the settlers. At two leagues we passed the mission of El Rosario,

in two more a small rancho dependent upon this mission, and six leagues farther on we camped near the Cunillo arroyo. To the right was El Capitán rancho situated on the bank of the San Antonio river ten leagues away from the presidio. In the last distance we crossed two nameless creeks, formed by the freshets from the hills.

On the 13th we traveled ten leagues southwest over land like the preceding. We crossed the arroyo of El Cunillo and shortly afterward that of Las Fuentecitas. El Agua Dulce arroyo was situated two leagues from the first and eight from Las Nueces river. We camped on the left bank of Las Nueces among thick trees. The rest of the day we employed in gathering dry logs to make rafts.

On the 14th we crossed the river on a raft composed of five logs tied together along their length by a cord and a few branches on top. Four more were made with as many cow-hides, on which all the baggage was taken over. The narrowness of the river, which was only fourteen to sixteen *toesas* wide, made it possible for us to cross over many times. The crossing concluded, we continued on our way west-northwest through a wooded section and a plain where there is a lagoon. Near the lagoon we camped on a small hill one eighth of a league from the river.

On the 15th we traveled twelve leagues southwest over gentle hills with much mesquite, wild cane, nopal, and a great deal of grama grass. We traveled on at a league's distance from Las Nueces river which, deviating to the north, then flows east. At five leagues we crossed the arroyo Blanco and at four leagues and a half from this came to Las Tablitas. A league and a half farther on is Los Olmitos arroyo where we camped on the other side of a large pond which was produced by freshets and circled by cottonwoods. This last distance is over very loose soil which is impassable when it rains and very difficult in dry season because of the long stretches of dried mud. In the vicinity the most outstanding thing on the north is the entrance of El Sacramento arroyo into Las Nueces river. Three leagues above the place where we crossed and toward the south the mesa of El Sancajo is visible. About eight leagues northwest there are some rather high hills, at the base of which the Frío river flows and, in the immediate vicinity, unites with Las Nueces on its left bank.

On the 16th we traveled fourteen leagues southwest over level land with some lowhills, all covered with abundant pasture, nopal, and shrubs. At six leagues we came to San Joseph on the bank of Las Nueces river, which we followed for some distance. At another four leagues is La Retama pond and two farther on that of Los Palitos Blancos. One short league from the latter is El Prieto cañada. A small stream runs through it which is impassable in flood time. However, we passed through it, encountering an occasional swamp. It is a quarter of a league long and at the end of one league we camped on a small hill which had some pools of water at its base. Since we had several heavy rain-storms there was no lack of water on this journey.

On the 17th we traveled thirteen leagues southwest over land like the preceding. At half way we came to San Casimiro arroyo. In that neighborhood the captain of militia of Laredo has a small rancho where he raises many horses. Five leagues and a half farther is El Carrizo arroyo, and four more is that of Saladito, preceding two others without names. At three leagues more is that of El Pato where a road branches off to go to San Antonio de Béjar. There was nothing of interest in this day's journey except the prodigious multitudes of rattlesnakes which live in this country. In the vicinity some mountain chains are visible.

On the 18th we traveled twelve leagues southeast over rising hills covered with coarse grass, nopals, and mesquites. At eight leagues we crossed San Ignacio arroyo, the woods growing more dense as far as the town of Laredo. There is nothing worth noting except the Chacón arroyo near the town. The settlement is reduced to some sixty huts situated on both sides of the Río Grande inhabited by sixty armed settlers, commanded by a militia captain and subject to the governor of Nuevo Santander. The town is under his jurisdiction as well as the territory covered in the previous day's journey, counting from El Mesquite, at a short distance from this part of Las Nueces river. They are administered by a parish priest dependent upon the bishopric of Guadalajara.

To the Presidio of San Juan Bautista del Río Grande.

On the 19th we traveled four leagues northwest over level land and one small hill covered with grass, mesquites, and some shrubs. After we had crossed the river in a good canoe we saw that it is divided into two arms formed by an islet in a very wide and deep bed. The river bed fills up during the rains and during the winter when it snows in New Mexico, although in this part it is always full of water. At this place its course takes an easterly direction making many turns until it empties into the Gulf of Mexico approximately to the east one quarter southeast. This night we camped on the Prieto road. There is nothing particular to note except a sierra which stood out among the others to the west. At the end of that chain, to the south, is the noted Real de La Iguana and at the opposite extremity there is a settlement called La Punta de Lampazos, of which I shall speak when I describe the New Kingdom of León.

On the 20th we traveled fifteen leagues northwest over level land, wooded with mesquite, and occasionally a small hill. About a league away on the right a chain of moderately high mountains was always visible. At its foot the Río Grande flows drawing nearer each time to the road until

it reaches the rancho of Joaquín Galán which is on its very
bank. It then draws off again and forms an arc until it has
passed El Toro arroyo. Here we terminated the day's
journey and camped near this arroyo. Two leagues from
our starting place are the ranchos of Blas María, where
the boundaries of the colony of Nuevo Santander have
recently been extended. Formerly they reached only to El
Carrizo Prieto. Entering the district of the presidio of San
Juan Bautista, Province of Coahuila, we came to Ramírez
arroyo at four leagues. We crossed with difficulty because
its banks had been washed out and made precipitous by the
last freshet, but it only had a few pools of water. Four
leagues from this is the rancho of Joaquín Galán. Two
leagues beyond is that of the curate of Laredo on a small
hill on the other side of Agua Verde arroyo whose bed is
as wide and deep as that of a copious river, although it
only had one very large pool of water. Three leagues beyond is that of El Toro. All these ranchitos consist of small
huts and a very few people who are occupied in caring for
many flocks and herds of goats. The principal commerce
of the whole colony consists of mules, horses, and goats,
with but little reliance on crops. Few are planted and they
are so neglected that they scarcely meet the needs of the
country.

On the 21st we traveled twelve leagues northwest over
very high steep hills. At one short league is the arroyo
Blanco. Three leagues farther is that of Las Iglesias. In
this stretch there are some sandy sections and others that
are rocky, which make the road difficult. Two leagues farther on is Las Animas arroyo and four beyond it El Amole
arroyo on whose upper banks are several little ranchos. At
a distance of two leagues from this crossing we camped on
the opposite bank of El Agostadero arroyo. There are
only puddles in all these arroyos and in the vicinity near

the arroyo of Las Iglesias are rocks resembling ruins of buildings.

On the 22nd we traveled five leagues in the same direction and over land like the preceding, passing by the summer pasture of Rositas de San Juan, through which a little stream flows. Two leagues from the presidio is Castaño arroyo which we crossed at La Laja ford. From its neighborhood we were accompanied by a crowd of mission Indians who went along on foot and on horseback, shouting and yelling discordantly in our honor.

Before burying ourselves again in the district of Coahuila I shall give a detailed description of the province of Texas and I shall say something of the colony of Nuevo Santander, although briefly since I saw only a small strip of it and that only in passing, even though little trouble and time are needed to get full information about it.

DESCRIPTION OF THE NEW KINGDOM OF
THE PHILIPPINES OR PROVINCE OF TEXAS

This province is situated between 26° and 34° north latitude and between 275° and 286° longitude, computed from the meridian of the island of Santa Cruz de Tenerife. It is bordered on the east by Louisiana, the boundary line being the Río San Andrés de los Caudachos or Riviére Rouge. The presidio of Nachitos, belonging to the French, is located there and is seven leagues away from our presidio at Los Adaes. On the west are the provinces of Coahuila and Nuevo Santander. On the other sides are savage tribes. They are troublesome only at San Antonio de Béjar and its vicinity. Because they are allied with the Texas, they never molest the presidio of Los Adaes, in whose vicinity they live.

The temperature of this country ranges to extremes of heat and cold. The rivers and arroyos which I have mentioned in the diary are impassable when it rains. When it is dry they have little or no water and, as their beds are too deep, they are unsuitable as a source of water supply. Therefore, they cannot be counted upon for the establishment of settlements, much less as the irregularity of the rains does not permit the growing of seasonal corn, except in some years. Besides this, there are so many flies of various kinds, horse-flies, ticks, mites, and various other insects that they make it uninhabitable. In some places the women become sterile, as happened to those at the presidio of La Bahía when it was located for a time on the banks of the Río Guadalupe. This is the reason why the immense distance between San Antonio de Béjar and the vicinity of Nacogdoches is inhabited during the winter only by numberless bear, coyote, deer, and bison. Nor can many birds live there, with the exception of wild turkeys which travel in flocks and many owls, whose cry suits perfectly the lugubrious nature of the country. The unending forest of pine, live-oak, and oak makes it more dismal. The trees are so tall and thick that in some places it is difficult to see the sky. Moreover, there are immense numbers of walnut, mulberry, plum, chestnut, and medlar trees which offer a supply of wild fruit to travelers. There are also grapes on the innumerable vines which climb around the trees. The sameness of the terrain, composed of low hills with no mountains, is not particularly agreeable to the sight.

The only population consists of the presidios of San Antonio, Bahía, Orcoquizac, and Los Adaes, together with the nearby missions of which I have already spoken. All the rest of this province and its surrounding country is occupied by the movable villages of the following savage Indian nations: Adaes, Ais, Ainais, Nacogdoches, Neches, Nazones, Nabidachos, Naconomes, Tojuanes, Anames, Ervipiames, Cujanes, Mayeyes, Pampopas, Pasúas, Cocos, Coapites, Copanes, Carancaguaces, Tacames, Taranames, Atastagonias, Pelones, Salinas, Parchinas, Annas, Pacaos, Pajaloce, Petalac, Orcoquizaes, Vidais, Atacapás, Apilusas, Borrados, Tancahues, Taguacanas. Further north are the Taguayas and Yscanis. They live together in a settlement called the Fort where the French go in canoes to trade by way of the Río Nachitos, or upper Colorado. They supply them with arms, powder and shot and through them the Comanches receive supplies in exchange for many deer skins. This is harmful to us because those arms are used against the presidios of San Sabá and New Mexico.

All these tribes are allied with the Texas Indians and our safety in that province is entirely dependent upon their fidelity. They have little respect for the Spanish and we are admitted only as friends, but without any authority. A very convincing proof of this is that we found a Spanish girl a slave of the Texas Indians in the San Pedro village and neither the so-called authority of the Nation nor money could liberate her. How disrespectful to the honorable forces of his Majesty, supposed to maintain law and order! Here they are in the shameful position of supplicants, even though the whole country is not worth one year's allotment of funds! And now it is worth less to us since his Majesty is in possession of Louisiana, including the presidio of Nachitos. From here, if so desired, the exposed missions of Nacogdoches, Ais, etc., could be protected, thus avoiding the expense of the company at Los Adaes and its governor. The town of San Antonio de Béjar could be added to Coahuila and Orcoquizac and Bahía could be abandoned. The few Indians from the missions of the latter could be transferred to San Antonio where there is more than enough room for them. This would result in a considerable saving without losing any of the so-called control of this province.

The colony of Nuevo Santander extends from Laredo following the course of the Río Grande del Norte to the Gulf of Mexico, as shown on the general map. Its climate is hot, as it is all along that coast, and its inhabitants, few in number, support themselves by their trade in horses, mules, and goats. They spend little time on their crops, for which reason they have little corn. Their proximity to the Sierra Madre, inhabited by several savage tribes, exposes them to frequent attacks. For this reason several squads are maintained at various places to protect them.

On the 22nd [of November], as I have said, we arrived at the presidio of San [Juan] Bautista del Río Grande, situated at 28°35′ north latitude and 272°5′ longitude, computed from the Tenerife meridian. Its cavalry company is composed of 33 men, including the captain, lieutenant, and one sergeant. Its annual allotment amounts to 10,245 pesos. Moreover, each soldier, including the lieutenant, is given six pounds of gunpowder, as is the practice in all the presidios which his Majesty has on the frontier. There are also forty settlers with their families. Many have left to settle at La Babia and the new town of San Fernando because of lack of farm land which has been taken over by the nearby missions of San Bernardo and San Juan Bautista. The first has 101 families, and the second 33 families from the various tribes mentioned in the description of this province. Among them are many Borrados, who are still savages. From both missions 170 men could be armed, some using bows and arrows, some pikes, half-moons [*medias lunas*], and a few, shotguns. The spiritual care of these people and the administration of the presidio is entrusted to three priests from the College of Our Lady of Guadalupe of Zacatecas. They receive an annual stipend of 450 pesos each.

To the Sabinas River.

On the 30th we set out for the city of Monterrey. We traveled eight leagues south over level country with some low hills and covered by a low growth of mesquite, huizaches, cat's claw, etc. At two leagues we crossed the Castaño arroyo. Four leagues from it we crossed the Amole, and two leagues from the latter, that of Juanes. The water stands in pools at intervals. We camped close to a small rancho on the banks of this creek. There is nothing of note in the vicinity except a low range which runs north and south to the west of the road as far as San Diego, whose name it bears. The range begins at a place called Calzones, and passes by Peyotes where there are two missions, protected by the presidio of Río Grande. There are many Indians of various tribes living at these missions which are called the Dulcísimo Nombre de Jesús and San Francisco Bizarrón. A small pueblo is located near the latter at a place called El Carrizo. Here many of the Julimeños who fled from Julimes in Nueva Vizcaya have gathered. All of this is administered by a Franciscan father.

DECEMBER

On the 1st we traveled fourteen leagues south over country the same as that of the previous day. The high sierras of La Candela, La Punta, and Carrizal, parts of the Sierra Madre, follow the cordillera of San Diego. At the foot of the first-named is La Carroza pass, used when traveling to Monclova, which is eighteen leagues from La Candela mission. It can be identified by a hillock in the form of a circular tower, southwest one quarter south of the place called El Charco del Pescado, where we camped. From here the other sierras continue, inclining toward the east. On the road in a low place are several small nameless lagoons which dry up, as does the pool where we camped. In between, four leagues from the former, are the Magueyitos, with nothing of note in the vicinity except the Río de la Candela, which flows at the base of the sierra of the same name.

On the 2nd we traveled ten leagues south over country like that of the preceding day. After traveling four leagues, we passed the small lagoon of Juan Sánchez, and three leagues from this Las Salinitas lagoon. After still another three we arrived at the Sabinas river. We could not ford it at La Laja, since it was in flood. We were forced to go down river two leagues to Villarreal ford where we crossed in a small canoe between the junction of El Loacan arroyo and the Candela river with the Sabinas, that of the former being one league to the right and that of the latter one league to the left.

JURISDICTION OF THE NEW KINGDOM
OF LEÓN

To Estancia El Palo Blanco.

On the 3rd [of December] we traveled nine leagues south one quarter southwest over country similar to that of the preceding day. After six leagues we crossed the Candela river in shallow water near San Joseph rancho. Three leagues from this is the settlement called La Punta de Lampazos, where we stopped. This belongs to the New Kingdom of León whose jurisdiction begins on the right bank of the Candela river and follows its course as far as the Sabinas river. The other side is Coahuila. This town is composed of some Cuervo Indians and forty families of civilized people who have settled there. There is an alcalde mayor and a parish priest who look after them.

On the 4th we traveled fourteen leagues, the first eight south to the hacienda of El Carrizal, during which we twice crossed the little Presa river, with the Mesa de los Catujanes a short distance to the right. This consists of a hill steep on all sides with only one ascending path. On top is a plain five leagues long and from one-half to a league and a half wide and having various irregularities. Here there are many herds, kept locked up by their owner who had constructed a gate. It is said that last year's rains cut two or three paths at different places in the cliff, which had washed away. From La Punta one proceeds through country surrounded by lofty sierras and from El Carrizal one goes through a heavily wooded valley about three or four leagues wide formed by a continuation of those sierras. After traveling six leagues south-southeast through the valley, we camped at Lagunillas. Along the road we encountered several washed out gullies and some loose rocks.

In the vicinity to the right a short distance from **Carrizal**, the San Jerónimo pass can be seen. Some two leagues to the east is the horse ranch of Golondrinas under the jurisdiction of Carrizal.

On the 5th we traveled twelve leagues south one quarter south-east over country more cut up by gullies and more rocky than before, especially from Tlaxcala to Palo Blanco. After covering the first league we came upon a small pueblo of Tlaxcalteca Indians, called Boca de Tlaxcala, to the west of La Boca pass, from which it took its name, and where the river has its source. The river, after passing by this pueblo, flows to the mining town of Boca de Leones, three leagues away. Its waters irrigate all that country, which produces much corn, some grapes, and various other fruits. This mining town now has only a small population because of the decadence of the mines which are of low grade. Its temporal government is in the hands of an alcalde mayor, and the spiritual, of a parish priest. There is a hospice of *padres crucíferos*, in which there is only one priest and one friar. From this mining town the valley widens out till beyond Potrero there is an hacienda producing much sugar cane and corn, these being watered by a spring in the Candela range. After passing this hacienda the valley again narrows as far as the place called Palo Blanco. This road is very bad for vehicles on account of the many gullies, rocks, and thick woods which hamper passage, and the multitude of arroyos with very poor fords. The distance from the mining town to Potrero is two leagues, and from the latter to the horse ranch of Palo Blanco is six.

To Monterrey and Saltillo.

On the 6th we traveled twelve leagues in the same direction over country somewhat better than the previous day, but otherwise of the same kind and through the same valley. After traveling six leagues we reached the Mamulique hacienda, with a population of five hundred persons. They raise mules, horses, and cattle of all kinds, maize which they need for their own consumption, and sugar cane. Since the temperature does not permit the cane to reach the full maturity necessary to produce sugar they make a raw sugar loaf called *piloncillo*. Four leagues from this hacienda there is another, now in ruins, called San Diego where there were formerly several very rich mines. At the foot of it runs an arroyo of the same name. Twelve leagues farther on is Salinas, a small settlement of civilized people governed by an alcalde mayor and administered by a parish priest.

On the 7th we traveled ten leagues south and southeast through the said valley with the same woods as on previous days, although with a much better road. At the outset we crossed the river of the same name at the foot of the hill where the town is located. The river was quite wide and with water up to a horse's belly. Four leagues beyond is La Pesquería arroyo and four leagues farther we came upon La Estancia, two leagues this side of the city of Monterrey. We found several small ranchos in this stretch. This city is situated at 26°4′ north latitude, and 211°25′ longitude, by the Tenerife meridian. Its size and plan are accurately shown on the map I drew. In the vicinity, which this map did not include, the most noticeable things are the sierras surrounding it. Among these the best known are those of El Topo to the northeast in which there are several hot and cold water springs. To the south runs the Sierra Madre, very high and rugged, with a canyon to the west and southwest between it and Las Mitras sierra, situated to the west, through which one reaches Saltillo. From the latter the Santa Catalina river flows near the south side of the city and turns in an easterly direction. The arroyos of Mederos and La Estanzuela form the

Silla river and join the Santa Catalina five leagues east of the town, passing Cadereita. Later the river is joined by one which flows from La Boca de Guajuco and others until it reaches the Pilón mission. Of these the Pesquería and Salinas, after they unite, take the name of San Juan. To the east is the Cerro de la Silla and at the foot of this, to the north of the city, is the valley through which we entered. In all these sierras there are signs of many mines formerly worked, but tests made of them recently show that they are not of sufficiently high grade to cover expenses. The citizenry of this city and of the eight haciendas in its jurisdiction consists of five hundred families of Spaniards, mestizos, and mulattoes, including those of the company composed of three officers, one sergeant, and twenty-two soldiers. With its chaplain this entails an annual expense of 6,000 pesos to his Majesty. The governor also resides there, his salary being 3,300 pesos annually.

On the 21st we departed from Monterrey for Saltillo through the canyon already mentioned. It lies to the west southwest, and following this direction we traveled twelve leagues over very rocky country from Las Cruces. At the end of the first league one fords the Santa Catalina river in considerable water. Four leagues from the latter is the rancho of the same name, producing much maize and sugar cane. Some three leagues farther is Las Cruces. Immediately following there is a low rise forming a pass whose summit is called El Alto de las Encinillas. This is at two leagues. From here it is two more leagues to La Rinconada where there are two huts but, as they were not large enough to lodge us, we were obliged to camp. The two families inhabiting them occupy themselves in growing corn for their own use and in raising goats.

At this place the Monterrey squad was first stationed. It was raised to prevent the continual murders and robberies being committed in this valley by the Pelones Indians, together with other tribes who made their entry through two other canyons. One was very narrow and ran from El Pilón through the Sierra Madre. The other serves as the bed of the Pesquería Grande river, which flows through it from El Saltillo and is completely boxed in.

On the 22nd we traveled twelve leagues southwest. At one quarter league we found the road full of rocks and gullies and for quite a distance it followed the river bed which, as I mentioned above, comes from Saltillo. The road is most difficult until it begins to climb some hills. These are not very rugged and are called Cuesta de los Muertos because they are dotted with crosses for the graves of the many men killed there by the enemy Indians. The highest point is some two leagues from La Rinconada. From there it descends one league, almost imperceptibly, through several small hills over bad terrain to El Muerto arroyo. Along the banks and bed the road runs as far as the rancho of Ojo Caliente, which is situated on its banks. Leaving this on the right, the road runs through country more open and level as far as Saltillo, a distance of seven leagues. In this stretch are several haciendas and ranchos, the principal ones being Los Migueles, on the arroyo of the same name, and Los Rodríguez, two leagues before reaching the town. The town is also preceded by an arroyo with a very deep bed but little water and by a copious ditch capable of irrigating all this countryside. This last bit of road was in very bad condition from the rains. In the whole country from Monterrey to Saltillo there is no pasturage, this arid land producing only brush, mezquite, nopal, wild lettuce, and palms.

DESCRIPTION OF THE NEW KINGDOM
OF LEÓN

It is situated on the eastern side of the Sierra Madre called the Sierra Gorda and it extends along it approximately north south from 23° to 28° north latitude and from 270° to 272° longitude, computed from the Tenerife meridian. It is surrounded by the jurisdictions of Coahuila, Colonia, Nueva Galicia, and Vizcaya, as will be seen on the general map. Its settlements are the city of Monterrey which is the capital, the four towns of San Felipe de Linares, San Gregorio de Cerralvo, San Juan de Cadereita, and the town of Horcasitas or Punta de Lampazos; the mining towns of Boca de Leones, Sabinas, Iguana, and San Carlos de Vallecillo, together with several haciendas dependent upon these jurisdictions in the valleys of the Río Blanco, Salinas, Carrizal, Santa Catalina, Pesquería Grande, Guajuco, and El Pilón. The number of families, Spanish, mestizo, and mulatto, amounts to 3,050, under the care of parish priests subject to the bishopric of Guadalajara. In the two pueblos of Tlaxcaltecas, one in the vicinity of Monterrey, and the other near Boca de Leones, named San Miguel de Aguayo, there are two hundred families. In the two missions of Purificación and Concepción situated in the valley of El Pilón, the pueblo of San Cristóbal de los Gualagüises, and the district of La Punta there are five hundred persons of the following Indian tribes: Bocarros, Xanambres, Gualagüises, Borrados, Pelones, Pajuamas, Xalayas, Malahuecos, Pitisfiafiles, Guachinochiles, Talaguichis, Alazapas, and Paxaltoes. They are administered by Franciscan fathers and all are subject to a governor whose jurisdiction is under the captaincy general.

The climate of this province tends to be hot, as its situation between sierras deprives it of free ventilation. For this reason it produces various fruits characteristic of hot countries, plenty of sugar cane, and much corn and beans. Many horses and cattle of all kinds are raised, this being its principal industry. Some silver is taken from the mines mentioned above, but their ores are low grade, the best being that of El Vallecillo, which is being actively worked at present. The great numbers of mines found all over those mountains are of that same kind and even inferior and hence they are neglected.

As regards wild animals, game, fish, and insects found there, this province is identical with Coahuila. Its proximity to the Sierra Madre exposes it to some attacks from the Indians of the tribes above mentioned who take refuge there. In the vicinity of the Río Blanco the Siguis and the Siguillones commit hostilities frequently. Their number, judged from those seen in war, is supposed to be about a hundred bowmen. They usually enter by the Cuesta de San Antonio and destroy the haciendas in this valley.

To the Hacienda de Cedros.

On the 28th [of December] we left Saltillo for Zacatecas. We traveled eight leagues by the same road which we had traveled on the sixth of June, to the San Juan de Vaquería hacienda where we stopped.

On the 29th we traveled sixteen leagues south over level, arid country. At first the road passes through a valley of varying widths for a distance of four leagues until it reaches a small slope called El Portezuelo and enters a plain nearly circular whose diameter must be about four leagues. It is bounded on all sides by high rugged sierras, except on the northeast where there is an opening, through which the whole country can be seen as far as the horizon. We came out through a wood and one league from the same we came upon the rancho of La Punta nine leagues from San Juan de la Vaquería where there is only a well of brackish water and a pool of rain water. We passed two plains connected by a canyon. At the end of the latter we found, about a quarter of a league to the right of the road, the pasturage of Canutillo on the slope of some hills near a small spring of very good water whose overflow runs into a pool and serves to water the few cattle and goats that can stand the aridity of that land.

On the 30th we traveled eight leagues south and then crossed the Canutillo pass. It is short and without difficulty except for a brief, steep incline of solid rock at its highest point where the road turns west. After going through another small pass at a distance of a half-league, a narrow valley leads west one quarter southwest and widens near the hacienda of Cedros situated at the foot of some low hills where silver is mined. We passed Mazapil on the left. At the top of the Canutillo pass another road branches off to the Bonanza hacienda which is only one-half league to the south. There some fairly good silver mines are worked and the ores smelted. Mining, farming, and other occupations account for a population of two thousand souls. Five leagues to the west on the other side of a cordillera is the mining town of Mazapil. Notwithstanding the decadence of its mines, there are a number of people who are governed by an alcalde mayor.

The hacienda of Cedros has a larger population than that of Bonanza. Besides various grains, it produces very good grapes, from which a red wine is made, the best in America. To the west, at a distance of some ten leagues, one may see a hill higher than any other in this vicinity and with a hummock in the center called Teria peak.

To Zacatecas.

On the 31st [of December] we traveled twelve leagues principally south over level country with much gravel and as arid as those of the previous days. There were no pastures nor other products except an abundance of herbs called *gobernadora*, wild lettuce, palms, and some zaguaros. Various sierras are to be seen in all directions. We stopped at some huts called El Potrillo. There are people there while the water lasts. This is caught in a pool which serves to water some herds, the only possessions of this small rancho. One league before reaching this, we passed the small Calzones hill.

Although the haciendas of Bonanza and Cedros have not been included in the territory of Nueva Galicia, they also belong to it.

JANUARY, 1768

On the 1st we traveled eight leagues south over country similar to that of the preceding day. At the end of the first two leagues is the Gruñidora hacienda, which consists of some six or eight huts and a very few people. For the other six leagues the country varies, the road going through some hills so low that the rises are barely noticeable. In these the ground is of gravel and there are also some pastures. The sierras roundabout are at a much greater distance, while to the east and west none are to be seen. At Gruñidora there is a spring with water which is not drinkable, especially by animals, and at San Ignacio there is only one pool. This small rancho comprises three or four huts with as many families, who take care of some horses and goats, of which there is a very small number, although the land is suitable for large numbers of sheep and cattle, etc.

On the 2nd we traveled fifteen leagues south over country similar to that of the day before. At the end of the first five leagues there are two adjacent ruined wells, the first called Zambrano and the second Concepción. The former is at the entrance of a small valley, formed by two chains of low, smooth hills which continue for two leagues as far as the Compromiso pass, which is a small rise through a very low hill. It leads to a plain from which the sierras can be seen only at a great distance. All the rest of the country is rolling hills for the eight leagues from this pass to the pasturages called Pozos de San Benito and Sierra Hermosa. Their population consists of five hundred persons who are employed in taking care of one hundred and nine thousand head of sheep which graze on the immense plains providing the pasturage. There is a great deal of grama grass, mesquite, cat's claw, tasajos, and some other shrubs or thickets. The same is true along the road, with nothing of note except the Pinto lagoon which is usually dry. This is one league before reaching the hacienda where water is drawn from a well and some pools or ponds.

On the 3rd we traveled seven leagues south one quarter southwest over country similar to that of the preceding day. At a distance of one league is the pasturage of San Miguel del Pozo Blanco, where there are four hundred people employed in caring for eighty thousand head of sheep, which graze on the plains thereabout. Four leagues beyond is the place called Santa Rita, where there are two families living in two small houses and supporting themselves by making charcoal. Two leagues from here is El Vidrio lake, which, although quite large, usually dries up by February. To the east of this can be seen the sierra where the jurisdiction of Charcas begins.

On the 4th we traveled fourteen leagues south-south-west over very low hills like those of the preceding days. At two leagues there are some lime-kilns where there are three or four little houses belonging to the workmen. This place is called San Joseph and is on the bank of a quite large lagoon. At this place there are two roads. We left the one on the right which goes by San Cosme and Rayón to Zacatecas and took the other without noting anything special as far as the Gutiérrez valley. Leaving the road we traveled a quarter of a league to the right to the Gutiérrez hacienda which is surrounded by several little houses whose few inhabitants are employed in taking care of some horses and mules pastured in the vicinity. We also had on our right a road to El Fresnillo, seven leagues from our starting place. There was nothing remarkable to be seen except the Cerro de Santiago on our left twenty leagues from Zacatecas.

On the 5th we traveled six leagues south-southwest over low hills somewhat more rugged than the preceding with several ravines and rougher footing because of the prevalence of gravel. At four leagues we came to an arroyo with a small amount of water running in a wide deep bed. On its high bank opposite, the Guerreros hacienda is situated. It has some small houses and a rather large chapel. Only a few people live here. At one league is the Colegio de Nuestra Señora de Guadalupe of the Franciscan fathers of the *propadanda fide*. One league farther is the city of Zacatecas. By another horse trail which leads over the hills to the said city a league is saved.

To the Pueblo Guajoquilla La Alta.

On the 13th we set out from Zacatecas for Nayarit. We traveled ten leagues west-northwest, the first five by way of the Maguey plain. About halfway the road to Fresnillo branches off to the right. At the end of the said plain is the hacienda which gives it its name. There remain five long leagues to Los Órganos cattle ranch. The road is full of gravel and passes over some low hills. There is only a short stretch of rocky road descending one of the hills half a league before the said cattle ranch. Everywhere near the road one sees several hills covered with good pasture. At the Maguey hacienda and the dependent Los Órganos cattle ranch more than 100,000 head of sheep are raised, as well as a great many cattle and some horses. Near this cattle ranch one sees mountains resembling organ pipes. The place takes its name from these mountains.

On the 14th we traveled eleven leagues west-southwest. At the start there were low hills which become progressively higher. In three leagues ones comes to the little ranchos of San Juan de la Ermita. They are situated in a little valley where a small stream flows. Four leagues beyond one climbs the slope of Las Quatro Mangas, which, with its descent of about the same length, composes half a league. One immediately faces a rather high sierra which we skirted for a short distance until we entered the mouth of the Quelite valley. We traveled these three leagues to the San Antonio de la Sauceda hacienda situated in a hollow surrounded by mountains. There are two openings through which the Sauceda river flows. This river rises in some small springs in the sierra of Quatro Mangas and directs its course west, passing through the said valley.

Eight leagues to the south of San Juan de la Ermita is the town of Jerez with the jurisdiction over the former.

At the San Antonio de la Sauceda hacienda there are 18,000 sheep and a thousand horses. Crops are also planted and they sometimes raise as much as twenty *fanegas* of corn, but not often, on account of the early frosts. Five leagues to the northwest is the *condado* of San

Mateo which includes several haciendas where cattle and horses are raised.

On the 15th we traveled seven leagues southwest, the first two over hills like those of the preceding day, to the Lobatos cattle ranch, dependent on that of San Mateo. The mesa of the same name extending over four leagues has two lagoons with some little houses nearby which shelter the people who look after cattle in that neighborhood. In a narrow and very deep valley the hacienda of San Agustín is located, and one league beyond it that of Nuestra Señora de la Concepción del Valle del Valparaíso. As it is a capital, a lieutenant alcalde mayor lives there, subject to Jerez. There is also a curate, dependent on the bishopric of Guadalajara. It has some farm land, some horses, cattle, and sheep. As many as two hundred persons are employed. It is situated on the bank of the same river which passes through La Sauceda. The waters of this river are increased by another stream which comes from San Mateo five leagues away and which joins it a short distance from the town. The products and people of the hacienda of San Agustín are the same as those I have just mentioned.

On the 16th we traveled fourteen leagues southwest over very high but less rugged sierras. But the road was impracticable for wagons and after going three leagues we left them at La Concepción. A quarter of a league to the left of the road, following the deep bed of an arroyo, we came to a little hill where we found a farm called El Astillero. From it we began the ascent of the Sacramento range. After traveling over several slopes and uneven ground of its flat summit for six to seven leagues we descended to a valley where the ranchos of Buena Vista or Perales and Maderas are situated. One league from the latter is Guajoquilla la Alta, Indian pueblo of the district of Colotlán. The population exceeds 1,500 persons, including 500 warriors and some civilized people. They are

administered by a parish priest and governed by a deputy
magistrate placed there by the captain of that district
under whose charge are the thirty-two well populated Indian pueblos which compose it. Two leagues to the east of
this pueblo is the San Antonio hacienda, which, with four
other pueblos, recognizes the superior government of the
lieutenant of Guajoquilla.

To the San Juan Peyotán.

On the 17th we did not travel. On the 18th we traveled
sixteen leagues principally southwest over a very rough
mountain range. We began the three-league climb from
Guajoquilla to the troublesome and rough descent of El
Zapote. The latter ends in an arroyo of the same name.
On its bank is the miserable little rancho of the same name.
El Muerto slope follows and is of the same nature as the
preceding. At two leagues is the small and dry El Muerto
arroyo. At a short distance we began the violent and deep
descent to the Chepelagana river which is two leagues
from that of El Muerto. This is a small river flowing
through a cañon beginning near the town of Nombre de
Dios and passing between two very high and rugged
mountain ranges. Its course is approximately south until it
meets the Santiago or Río Grande river which empties into
the Mar del Sur at Chilapa and San Blas. Then comes El
Carrizalillo slope. It is three leagues high and is the highest, steepest, and most difficult of all because the rocks
make the passage dangerous. Moreover, the path is narrow and passes along the edge of several precipices. The
numerous turns vary from a scant footing up to three feet
in width. Half-way up the mountain on one slope the road
levels off for a bit where there is a small stream which
gives the name to the slope. On its bank there is a small
rancho. From the summit the road for three leagues alter-
nates between ascents and descents of slight consideration

as far as El Jagüey where we camped. This place is named for a pond of water in an arroyo where the water lasts the year round.

On the 19th we traveled seventeen leagues southwest. The first eight were over the top of the mountains. The high ground leads into a plain with a gentle slope over land with good footing so that the descent is unnoticeable. It is covered with oaks and pines of medium height, and also there are some small hills and uneven ground from time to time until one reaches Los Incorporaderos which are on the other side of the summit. From here one has a clear view of El Tonatí mesa and many other mountains. Notwithstanding their great height they seem to form a valley between the two highest ranges of Los Incorporaderos and those situated on the other side of the mesa stretching to the north. In the first range are the pueblos of San Andrés Comata, Santa Catarina, and San Sebastián. These places are inhabited by the Guisoles Indians of the district of Colotlán. The insolence and pride of these Indians is unchecked in the inaccessible heights around Los Incorporaderos. At the beginning of the Alacranes slope to the right and near the road is El Angel spring. Three leagues down the slope is the Alacranes arroyo. For four leagues beginning from this arroyo to La Piedra China there is a constant descent, although several ascents and descents occur alternately. These continue up to the little rancho of El Pastor. The road passes over several very steep slopes. Among these the most dangerous, because of its precipices and the narrowness of the path, is the one called La Puerta. It was the only pass until recently when another road was opened from the top of a slope between the Alacranes and La Piedra China. This road, turning to the right, goes to San Juan Peyotán, to which belongs the little rancho El Pastor, so-called because it is situated at the foot of the hill of this name. The road on this day's journey

is full of loose stones and pointed rocks. The whole surrounding country is covered with a prodigious quantity of
pines and oaks, with much tall grass, not at all suitable for
feeding the horses. The great differences between the ele-
vations of the mountain summits and the depths of their
valleys produce diverse temperatures. On the heights it is
cold with corresponding products; while in the valleys
there are fruits which are produced only in hot countries.

To the Presidio of San Francisco Xavier de Valero.

On the 20th we traveled ten leagues principally southwest. The first three continued the descent of the preceding
day and were more level and had better footing as far as
the Santa Rosa arroyo which we forded in shallow water.
We then immediately climbed a rough but short slope, on
whose summit is La Primera Guerra, so-called because
there the Spaniards who conquered the province experienced the first opposition from these natives. This is the
only pass and is a gap 200 *toesas* wide between some steep
crags which surround the foot of the sierra bathed by the
arroyo. It permits no other ascent except by a very narrow
winding path leading to the said gap. The Indians built
a straight bulwark of loose stones across the gap which is
still well preserved and actually serves to shut off that territory used for pasturage. It is necessary to go through a
barrier of crossed sticks. In the shelter of this wall the
natives faced our troops, but after a short struggle they
abandoned it. Later another pass was discovered requiring
a long detour. This is useful to know because, if it should
be necessary to occupy this road again by force of arms,
the considerable bloodshed which the taking of this con-
stantly-defended post would cost, could be avoided by using the alternate route. The road then continues to the Río
de San Francisco or Jesús María one league away down a
slope with several sharp grades. On the left bank of the

river on a small rise the pueblo *de visita,* San Francisco, is situated. It is subject to the mission of Jesús María with a few Indians of the Cora nation. One league from it is the mission of Jesús María, on the left bank of the same river, which takes its name from that mission. The intervening territory is like the preceding with a precipice here and there making the narrowness of the road more terrifying. Quite a large number of Indians of the Tecoalmes nation compose this settlement. In it is a spacious church, very extensive government houses, and annexed to them is the habitation of the savage Indians of that nation. The employment of these buildings was judged to be necessary to subject the nation, according to reports of the Jesuit missionaries.

At the foot of the mission flows the river of the same name. The road continues partly through its bed and partly along the slope of the mountain. There are a number of precipices. It is necessary to ford the river five times more before coming to the Fraile arroyo two leagues away. This empties into the first named which goes on to join that of Santiago. The road continues through the cañada where the Fraile arroyo flows for about a league and a half, during which distance it must be forded several times before reaching the foot of the slope of the Tonatí mesa. The climb, including all the turnings, covered a league and a half. This includes all the difficulties, precipices, and crags which I have mentioned on the preceding days. The ascent terminates in two rocks which make a sort of door for entering the mesa. At the beginning there are small crags and afterwards one sees several hills rising in different places. Behind one of them which shows up to the southwest the presidio is situated. Nearby is a mission a league and a half from the entrance. This road is good, with the exception of a somewhat dangerous stretch of slope which one must cover before arriving. The garrison of the presidio consists of forty-three soldiers including the captain, a lieutenant, an alférez, and two sergeants. Their yearly allowance amounts to 13,910 pesos. This expense could be considerably diminished by reducing the company to a single squad of ten men and a corporal which would be sufficient for the support of the missionaries and to keep those natives, who are very docile, pacified.

FEBRUARY, 1768

To Guajoquilla La Alta.

On the 4th we set out from the presidio of San Francisco Xavier de Valero, doubling back to Guajoquilla la Alta by the San Juan Peyotán road. On our right we saw El Pastor two leagues away. After passing La Primera Guerra, one follows the Santa Rosa river bed up to a point where another creek joins it. Following the latter a short distance one comes to La Boquilla. From there to the mission of San Juan Peyotán, a league away, the road is almost level. The land is planted with maize, sugar-cane, and beans and is the richest in the province.

On the 5th we went to Jagüey which is an equal distance from the mission and from El Pastor. We chose, as the least dangerous, the road from Piedra China which has occasional precipices.

On the 6th we arrived at Guajoquilla.

DESCRIPTION OF THE NEW KINGDOM OF
TOLEDO OR THE PROVINCE OF NAYARIT

It is situated in the most rugged part of the Sierra
Madre between 21° and 23° north latitude and between
261° and 264° longitude, counting from the Santa Cruz
de Tenerife meridian. From north to south its borders are
the pueblo of Guasamota, belonging to Nueva Vizcaya,
and the Río Grande de Alicia, which divides it from the
district of Nueva Galicia. On the east it is terminated by
the Río de Atenco, otherwise Chepalagana, where the district of Colotlán begins. On the west its boundary is the
Río de San Pedro, which separates this district from the
district of Acaponeta. All this will be shown on the general
map. Also shown is the location of the seven missions of
Santísima Trinidad de la Mesa, Santa Teresa, San Juan
Peyotán, Jesús María, Guaynamota, San Pedro Yscatán,
and Nuestra Señora del Rosario, which, with their three
pueblos *de visita,* Santa Rosa, San Francisco de Paula, and
San Juan de Corapa, include 890 families of Choras and
Tecoalmes Indians, administered by the Franciscan fathers. Also shown is the pueblo of Santa Fé, which is the
head of two others called San Diego and San Juan Bautista, inhabited by fifty families of Indians and thirty of
civilized people. The above, with the two mining camps of
San Francisco Tenamach and Naguapán, having 510 families of all kinds of people, compose the entire population
of this province.

It enjoys two climates—cold on top of the mountains
and hot in the deep ravines. In each part their products are
typical of the climate. Taken altogether they are maize,
beans, pumpkins, watermelons, sweet potatoes, plantains,
peaches, wild plums, and white zapotes. Nature allows

only scant harvest of these crops but she has been prodigal in covering all this area with an immense forest of pines, oaks, live-oaks, white and black cottonwoods, cedars, palms, mesquites, and Brazil wood. Very good and tasty honey is also gathered among the brambles, where bees, smaller than those of Europe, make their combs. A great deal of beeswax is taken, but the natives there do not know how to use it. In these woods there are some deer and white wolves, the only wild animals that live in this province. There are few birds. Minerals are plentiful but they are of such poor quality that they can hardly be worked.

On the 7th we did not travel.

On the 8th we set out from Guajoquilla on the same road by which we entered. On the 10th we reached the Maguey hacienda. The total distance from the presidio amounts to 80 leagues and the land beginning at Guajoquilla belongs to the Kingdom of Nueva Galicia.

JURISDICTION OF NUEVA GALICIA

To Querétaro.

On the 11th we traveled sixteen leagues, the first four to the south as far as Calera; the next six to the east up to the hostel of Tlacotes; the remaining six to the San Diego hacienda to the southeast. All was over gentle rolling hills with some stretches of plain. They were covered with a great many prickly pears and plenty of pasture. There was nothing of note except a small hacienda called San Joseph de Tlacotes situated a league from the hostel at the outlet of a small valley. Between there and San Diego there were several widely separated small ranches. In the distance some low sierras could be seen.

On the 12th we traveled fifteen leagues principally southeast one quarter east over level land and some small rolling hills with many prickly pears and plenty of pasturage. At the end of the first nine leagues is the Ciénega Grande, an hacienda belonging to the Jesuits in which a great many horses and mules, and wheat and corn, are raised. It also has a stamp mill with five crushers, a number of *arrastres,* and everything else necessary for the reduction of silver with mercury. They bring the ore from a mine a league and a half away. It yields fourteen ounces per load. This is five above the cost, which is only nine. A reasonable profit might result if miners were employed in proportion to the quantity of ore in the mine. At present only a few people are employed just as in the other branches of the hacienda. Six leagues from this is Sauz Dorado, a half dozen huts, several of which are found on the road of this day's journey, and an hacienda a league and a half from San Diego.

On the 13th we traveled fifteen leagues, the first two east over level ground as far as Las Bocas de Gallardo where there are some little houses. A quarter of a league from them is a small slope, very bad because there is an outcropping of rocks. They may be avoided by taking the coach road which makes a detour of one league. A plain then follows for three leagues and a half as far as another slope one-eighth of a league long. This is not very steep but is annoying on account of many rocks. From this to Los Ojuelos hacienda there are two leagues of level ground. Of the same nature are the six remaining to Santa Efigenia rancho which lies southeast of Las Bocas. There is nothing worthy of note in its vicinity, the products of which are many prickly pears and abundant pasture.

On the 14th we traveled thirteen leagues principally southeast. At the end of the first eight is the small town of San Felipe, composed of Indians and some civilized people. Their houses, with the exception of some that are fairly good, are a group of scattered huts. This stretch is level, with some small hills, and in the vicinity there are several small lagoons, haciendas, and ranchitos, and an infinity of prickly pears. Of this same kind are the five leagues remaining to the Quemada hacienda, in which there are also some lagoons on whose banks are several ranchitos and haciendas, among them Las Trancas, El Pájaro, etc.

On the 15th we traveled fifteen leagues principally southeast. At the end of the first four is the dam. The water back of the dam forms a medium-sized lake and along its bank there are some houses. Two leagues farther is Dolores, an Indian pueblo, and at two more leagues is the hacienda de la R. Two leagues beyond is El Fuerte. These six leagues cover continuous hills and some stretches of loose rock. Still rougher hills and more rocks provide two leagues of very bad road leading to the Indian pueblo of Atotonilco. Two more, somewhat better than the latter, lead to the town of San Miguel El Grande. The principal direction of this journey was to the southeast, but in order to avoid some bad spots, the road makes a detour, taking different directions. In the vicinity are many prickly pears and some haciendas with a good deal of farm land.

On the 16th we did not travel.

On the 17th we traveled fourteen leagues principally southeast. At the start there is a very steep, long slope. Afterwards the road covers level ground for five leagues to the Nietos pass. There are some huts at the foot of the ascent which is very difficult. The descent on the other side is equally troublesome because of the many stones from there to the Buenavista hacienda two leagues away. There is a little improvement in the seven leagues from there to Querétaro.

On the 18th and 19th we did not travel.

On the 20th we set out from Querétaro and, after traveling a distance of forty-one leagues, we arrived at Mexico on the 23rd of the said month of February. We returned by the same road and places as when we set out, traveling the immense distance of 2,936 leagues, including the thirty that we traveled in exploration of the vicinity of Guajoquilla.

EXPLANATION

If one were to judge the character, number, and ferocity of the enemy Apache Indians by the constant killings, thefts, and outrages which they commit, his conclusion would be markedly erroneous. Moreover, in view of the scant success of the existing presidios, he would deem their increase indispensable in order to check these Indians. The lack of presidios, however, is not the cause of the impunity with which the Apaches commit their depredations and of their annihilation of the two most useful provinces, Sonora and Nueva Vizcaya. Hence, my fervent zeal in his Majesty's service and the public welfare will not permit to remain hidden the true motives which attribute such boldness to the Indians and render ineffective such a large number of companies as the King, my master, is maintaining at immense cost to guard the frontiers. That I may not feel the remorse of omission, permit me to suggest the means which seem to me to be the most efficacious for remedying the situation.

The extreme ignorance and gross inexperience of the captains from the beginning has resulted in a type of fighting ineffective in those areas. Their culpable indolence has established a regular custom of remaining quietly in the presidios, allowing the enemy to enter and leave at will and in safety. Moreover, so that no one could credit them with doing nothing but attending to their own interests, when they are informed that the enemy are out on a raid they go in pursuit of them well assured of not overtaking them; for, allowing some time for the news to come, and much more to collect the horses and provisions, it is impossible to get within sight of the Indians. This has always happened, notwithstanding repeated experience. Naturally a man, whose weight, with that of the offensive and defensive arms, comes to fourteen *arrobas,* and who is leading five or six horses for remounts, never can run as fast nor for so long a time as an Indian, whose arms and equipment increase his weight very little, and who can alternate between a number of horses and mules, in proportion to the number stolen. The soldiers obstinately pursue the Indians until their own animals are exhausted and rendered useless for a long time. Then they return as well satisfied as though they had punished the enemy. And if at times the Indians, trusting in the ruggedness of the mountains and the torpidity of our troops in them, make a stand and wait, it is seldom that they fail to defeat our men, who, being poorly instructed by their officers, attack without method or order. In the same way they take flight, leaving the bravest to be sacrificed, without command from their leaders who are not in the habit of giving any. Nor would the soldiers, scattered at will, be able to hear them in competition with the screaming barbarians. The two forces are all mixed up, and out of this enormous confusion our men usually get the worst of it. The greater number of the enemy, their skill in shooting their arrows, and their agility give them evident advantages over our side. Our soldiers cannot even take advantage of the first shot, because they are totally ignorant of how to handle a musket. This is the result of the lack of training that should be given to them by their officers, were it not for the fact that the latter are, for the most part, more ignorant and less accustomed to fighting than the men. From the above one deduces the indispensable necessity of giving them good teachers who will discipline these troops in the necessary subordination to their officers. At present they respect their officers very little. Sometimes the officers have to force them to carry out their decisions as to whether or not the enemy shall be

216 THE FRONTIERS OF NEW SPAIN

attacked. For this reason many attempts fail. They should teach them to fight together in order and in silence and to use firearms. These should be of uniform caliber, because when they differ it often happens that they cannot find the ball that fits. Finally, they should train them to fight on horseback, teaching them to use their swords. But especially they should be taught how to fight on foot, for when the enemy are attacked on the plains they do not wait to take a stand but seek shelter immediately in the rough hills, where they cannot be pursued except on foot.

The soldiers' ordinary procedure of marching without scouts to reconnoitre the country thoroughly, their stupidity in starting a fight in a defile without first occupying the heights, their manner of guarding the camp and the horse drove, and all their operations need more or less instruction and reform. The various disasters which they have experienced through their lack of preparations have taught them nothing. Moreover, the enemy knows perfectly well how to take advantage of this. The enemy are amazing in their conduct, vigilance, speed, order, and endurance when they are raiding and retreating with their prizes. They use stratagems which always deceive our men. But all their precautions cease the moment they think they are safe within the limits of their own territory. Since it is impossible to surprise or overtake them in our territory, why do we not invade theirs, where our troops have always been successful when they have entered in small detachments. On the contrary, when they made large noisy expeditions to the Gila province, they only frightened the game. I therefore judge, founding my opinion on these experiences and various other reflections, that the only method of terrorizing, subjecting, or even annihilating these Indians, if that should be necessary for the better service of his Majesty and the public good, is a continuous offensive war in their own territory. By this means they would be exterminated in a short time, simply by depriving them of their one means of subsistence, which is robbery. In addition, by making prisoners of the women and children their numbers would be diminished even though few braves or warriors were killed or taken prisoner.

INDEX

Pilón valley, N. L.: 195

Piloncillo: crude sugar, 192

Pima Indians: Pimas Bajos or Lower Pimas, 120, 129; Pimas Altos or Upper Pimas, 21, 107, 108, 111, 112, 113, 117, 118, 125, 127, 128, 129, rebellion in Sonora, 22, 126, 128

Pimería Alta, Son.: 14, 21, 125, 127

Piros Indians: 14, 93

Pitas Indians: 155

Pitic, Son.: 113, 129

Pitiqui, Son.: 22, 112, 128

Pitisfiafiles Indians: 195

Poarames Indians: 75

Poliachi, mining camp, Chih.: 132

Policarpio, Cajón de, Son.: 129

Population: Aguascalientes, 53; Alamo pueblo, 137; Alburquerque, 90; Altar, 112; Atotonilco, 66; Avino, 60; Bahía, 178; Buenavista, 120; Caborca, 112; Carmen hacienda, 18, 96; Chihuahua, 69; Coahuila, 154; Colotlán, 35; Durango, 59; El Gallo, 63; El Paso, 83; Espíritu Santo, 33; Fresnillo, 55; Fronteras, 104; Guajoquilla, 66; Guajoquilla la Alta, 203; Horcasitas, 25, 116; Indian, 23; Janos, 20, 100; Laredo, 34, 181; Mapula, 69; Mazapil, 198; Monclova, 142; Monterrey, 34, 193; Nayarit, 209; New Mexico, 90, 93; Nombre de Dios, 57; Nuestra Señora de Guadalupe, 68-69; Nuevo León, 195; Patos hacienda, 139; Pichera pueblo, 131; Punta de Lampazos, 190; Querétaro, 48; San Antonio de Béjar, 160; San Antonio de la Ramada, 67; San Bartolomé, 8, 66; San Buenaventura, 98; San Felipe, 90; San Fernando, 145; San Ignacio, 113; San Joseph de los Pimas, 118; San

Juan Bautista, 186; Sandía, 90; Santa Catarina, 60; Santa Fé, 91; Santo Domingo, 91; Sariqui, 111; Silao, 50; Suaqui, 120; Tecoripa, 119; Terrante, 20, 107; Tomé, 89; Tubac, 23, 109; Valle del Valparaíso, 203; Zacatecas, 55; Zarco de Arriba, 63, 64

Populo pueblo, Son.: ruined, 116

Portezuelo, Jal.: 52

Portezuelo (Capulín) pass, Coah.: 197

Potrero, N. L.: 191

Potrero, Son.: 127

Potrillo, Zac.: 199

Pozo Hediondo sierra: 76

Pozos de Calvo, Coah.: 136

Pozos de Trinidad, Son.: 129

Presa river, N. L.: 190

Presidios: 1, 4, 5, 6, 7, 8, 9, 11, 12, 13, 14, 16, 17, 18, 19, 20, 22, 24, 25, 26, 27, 29, 64, 66, 73, 76, 77, 91, 98, 100, 104, 107, 109, 112; Altar, 112; Buenavista, 26, 120, Cerro Gordo, 8, 135; chain of, 33; changes in locations, 38, 39; Coahuila province, 154; Conchos, 8, 9, 67; cordon recommended by Rubí, 37-38; El Gallo, 8, 9, 63; El Pasaje, 7-8, 61; Fronteras, 104; frontier institution, 23; Guajoquilla, 9, 66; Horcasitas, 25, 116; Janos, 20, 100; Loreto, 33, 177-178; Los Adaes, 32, 167; Mapimí, 8; Monclova, 28, 142; Monterrey, 34, 193; Orcoquizac, 32, 171; San Antonio, 30-31, 160; San Buenaventura, 18, 98; San Francisco Xavier, 35, 208; San Juan Bautista, 34, 187; San Sabá, 29-30, 151; Santa Rosa, 144; Terrenate, 20, 107; Tubac, 23, 109

Prieto cañada, Texas: 180

Prieto road, Tam.: 181